Val Pierce's passion for knitting began when her father taught her to knit at the age of five. She soon turned her talents to creating her own designs and since then has made a huge range of items, from evening dresses and baby bootees to teddy bears and rabbits. Val has authored numerous knitting books and her designs appear regularly in national knitting and crochet magazines. She lives and works in Shropshire, where she teaches knitting, as well as a range of other needlecrafts, to both adults and children.

Other Books by Val Pierce:

20 to Make: **Knitted Bears**
978-1-84448-482-9

20 to Make: **Knitted Mug Hugs**
978-1-84448-606-9

20 to Make: **Crocheted Bears**
978-1-84448-633-5

20 to Make: **Mini Christmas Crochet**
978-1-84448-740-0

20 to Make: **Knitted Baby Bootees**
978-1-84448-641-0

20 to Make:
Crocheted Granny Squares
978-1-84448-819-3

Little Christmas Decorations to Knit & Crochet
978-1-78221-129-7

Little Bears to Knit & Crochet
978-1-78221-008-5

KNITTED
Rabbits

Dedication

I dedicate this book to rabbit lovers
everywhere! May you find as much
joy knitting these little characters as
I had designing them.

KNITTED
Rabbits

20 easy knitting patterns
for cuddly bunnies

Val Pierce

Search Press

First published in 2015

Search Press Limited
Wellwood, North Farm Road,
Tunbridge Wells, Kent TN2 3DR

Text copyright © Val Pierce 2015

Photographs by Paul Bricknell at Search Press Studios

Photographs and design copyright © Search Press Ltd 2015

ISBN 978-1-84448-867-4

The Publishers and author can accept no responsibility for any consequences arising from the information, advice or instructions given in this publication.

Readers are permitted to reproduce any of the items in this book for their personal use, or for the purpose of selling for charity, free of charge and without the prior permission of the Publishers. Any use of the items for commercial purposes is not permitted without the prior permission of the Publishers.

Suppliers
If you have difficulty in obtaining any of the materials and equipment mentioned in this book, then please visit the Search Press website for details of suppliers:
www.searchpress.com

For further information, please visit the author's website:
www.crossedneedles.co.uk

Printed in China

Acknowledgements
Many thanks to Rico, Sirdar, Bergère de France and Patons, who were kind enough to supply their beautiful yarns for me to create some of the bunny rabbits.

Also thanks, as always, to Search Press for their kindness and understanding during the creation of the book, for their editing and wonderful photography, and for all the help and guidance given to me.

Last but not least, to my family and friends who have shown their support and encouragement whilst I was writing this book.

Contents

Jelly Bunnies, page 28

Fairy Bunny, page 46

Tweedy Bunny, page 70

Introduction

Knitting has been a passion for me since I was very young. Once I learned to knit as a little girl, I was always busy doing something – either knitting simple scarves or dolls' clothes. As I grew up I became more proficient and branched out into knitting more complicated projects. At first, toys were perhaps my least favourite things to knit, but once I had made a few I began to realise just how much fun they were to create – each one had its own special character and cute expression as it took shape. I am often asked if I ever run out of ideas for new toys but when I look at all the birds, animals j\jeptiles in the world I know that it will take me a very long time to run out of inspiration!

Rabbits are such cuddly creatures, with their delightful faces and floppy ears. I have designed twenty special bunny rabbits for this book, to please both young and old. They come in all shapes, sizes and colours. Some are tiny little bunnies that will sit in the palm of your hand, while others are big and cuddly. There are a few with cheeky expressions and some that are just plain in need of a hug or two. So why not have a go and make a whole collection of these cute characters for yourself and your family and friends?

Safety first

If you are making one of the rabbits for a child, you will need to be safety conscious. Some of the projects have embellishments, such as sewn-on buttons or pieces of felt, which could present a choking hazard, so substitute these for knitted or embroidered elements if you need to. If you intend to use safety eyes, these must be inserted before closing the head. Bear in mind that they can be a bit tricky to use – once in place they cannot be removed and changed around.

Stuffing

Making up your project will take time and patience to get right. Stuffing your toy is something that can either enhance or spoil the finished project, so take great care. The body, head, arms and legs all need to be stuffed to an equal density unless otherwise stated in the making-up instructions. Gently tease out the stuffing and use small amounts at a time, to create a smooth, even finish. Feet, paws, heads and noses also need to be shaped.

Last-minute checks

When you come to assemble your toy, check the following: are your sets of arms and legs equal in length and do they have the same circumference? Also check that the head and body look in proportion to each other – a huge fat body and a little tiny head, or vice versa, will spoil the look of your finished toy. Also, if your rabbit has clothes, check them against the stuffed toy before you sew it up. If you over-stuff him or her the clothes may not fit!

Finishing touches

Often the most difficult stage is the final one: adding the facial features. Experiment on a spare piece of fabric if you need to. It is important to try to get the eyes even and level. Rabbit noses are normally a 'Y' shape, but on some of the rabbits I have embroidered an oval shape using satin stitch. The mouth can be smiley or just straight. Experiment with your own ideas – you can always unpick and try again if you are not happy with the result. Don't be tempted to rush: all the time and care you take finishing off your project will be richly rewarded when you admire your completed toy.

Sewing

When sewing the head to the body, tack it in place first to ensure that it is level: if you position the head too far forward or back the toy will be unsteady. Once you are happy that it is in the correct position you can begin to sew. Take one stitch from the head and one from the body all around, pulling the yarn firmly. If need be, sew around the head again a second time to secure it. Pin the arms and legs in place before sewing, in exactly the same way, to check that you are happy with their position. Check whether your rabbit will be sitting or standing before you pin, so that you get the legs in the correct position.

Seams must be sewn very securely – remember, toys will be pulled and thrown around, and heads, legs and arms especially may get tugged a lot. There are many seaming methods that you can use, however the method you choose should depend on the type of yarn you have used, and the type of knitted fabric used in the project. I normally use a back stitch seam on stocking stitch, and edge-to-edge seam on garter stitch. Back stitch is a very strong seam, so works well for most toys.

Materials

The materials you will need to knit the rabbits in this book are listed here, along with a few notes to help explain how to use some of the yarns, needles and other equipment.

Yarns

I have used a wide variety of yarns, ranging from cashmere and silk 4-ply (fingering) yarns and wool DK (8-ply) yarns, to specialised fur fabric yarns. The textured yarns give a lovely realistic feel and look, but they are not always that easy to knit with as the fabric created is quite dense and counting stitches and rows can be quite tricky. All of the yarns can be substituted for a similar weight yarn as long as you follow the stated tension (gauge) for the specific design.

Knitting needles

You will need good-quality knitting needles in various sizes. Needles are a personal choice, so buy what you feel happy working with. I personally love wooden needles, which are comfortable to use and lightweight, but they can be very expensive to buy. If you are new to knitting I would suggest you choose a mid-price set of needles to start you off.

Stitch holders

It is sensible to have a couple of stitch holders as it is far easier to save unworked stitches on a holder than on a spare needle. A row counter is also a good idea when knitting with some of the fur yarns, as it can be easy to lose count.

Sewing needles

When making up the toys you will need a variety of sewing needles. Knitters' needles with large eyes are very useful when you have fur-type yarns to work with as they facilitate easier threading and sewing. Blunt-ended needles help when sewing seams as you will be less likely to split stitches. You will also need some sharp-ended needles for embroidering features and adding embellishments to your finished rabbits and their clothes.

Stuffing

Use a good-quality fibrefill safety stuffing for the rabbits. This will give a nice smooth, soft finish to your toy and is less likely to create lumps and bumps. It is of course fully washable, too.

Scissors

A good sharp pair of needlework scissors is invaluable. It makes it easy to cut close to the fabric when trimming yarn ends. As most of the rabbits have 'powder puff' tails you will need to make quite a few pompoms. Trimming these to a neat size is much easier with a pair of sharp scissors, although you could also buy a pompom maker.

Tape measure

A tape measure is very handy since you will need to measure tension (gauge) at the start of each project and also check lengths when making some of the clothes and accessories.

Buttons and embellishments

Some of the rabbits' outfits are embellished with buttons and beads, so make sure these are all securely attached. There is a great range of colours, shapes and styles available in craft stores or online. If you are making any projects with embellishments, don't give them to young children who may swallow or choke on any additional elements.

Knitting bag

Last but not least, it is sensible to have a work bag in which to keep all your yarns and needles safely tucked away while you are not using them. It will keep your work clean and also ensure that you don't lose anything you are working with.

Techniques

It is presumed that you have a basic knowledge of knitting and are proficient in casting on stitches, working knit and purl stitches and casting off finished pieces of knitting. A full list of abbreviations is given on page 96. However, for some of the projects in this book you will also need to be able to increase and decrease stitches, so here is some more guidance.

Increasing
Sometimes a piece of knitting requires shaping, which means that you will need to add stitches, or 'increase'. There are several easy-to-follow methods of producing increases.

Make one (m1)
With this method you pick up the horizontal strand between two stitches and knit or purl into it to form a new stitch.

Step 1: insert your left-hand needle from front to back under the horizontal strand between two stitches.
Step 2: knit or purl into the back of the strand on your left-hand needle.
Step 3: transfer the stitch onto your right-hand needle. The twist in the stitch prevents a gap from appearing in the work.

The bar method
This method produces a small horizontal stitch on the right side of the work. You knit into the front and back of a stitch to make two stitches. This type of increase in used on sleeve shaping or on pieces where the 'bump' will not matter.

Step 1: knit a stitch in the usual way but do not remove it from the left-hand needle.
Step 2: insert the right-hand needle into back of the same stitch and knit again.
Step 3: remove the stitch from your needle. The extra stitch formed by this method produces a small bump on the right side. It is not noticeable when worked on the edge of a piece.

Decreasing

Sometimes you will need to lose stitches in a row, in order to shape a piece of knitting. Casting off is the normal method used when more than three stitches need to be lost. However, if only one or two stitches have to be decreased, either of the methods described below can be used.

Knitting two stitches together

Right slant
Step 1: to make a right slant (k2tog), insert your needle in the next two stitches through the front of both loops. Take the yarn around the needle and draw it through.
Step 2: transfer the new stitch to your right-hand needle.

Left slant
Step 1: to make a left slant (k2tog tbl), insert your needle in the next two stitches through the back of both loops. Take the yarn around the needle.
Step 2: draw the thread through and transfer the new stitch to your right-hand needle.

Slipstitch decrease

This results in a slightly looser decrease than knitting two stitches together. When made on a knit row it slants from right to left and is abbreviated sl1, k1, psso. A similar decrease can be made on a purl row, when it slants from left to right. It is abbreviated sl1, p1, psso.

On a knit row
Step 1: slip one stitch knitwise from your left-hand needle onto the right-hand needle then knit the next stitch.
Step 2: insert your left-hand needle into the front of the slipped stich and pull it over the knitted one.
Step 3: the right-to-left slant made by this decrease in a knit row is used on the right side of the centre of the work.

13

Curly Bunny

This fluffy little fellow makes a great cuddly companion for a child of any age. Choose a fashion fur yarn to give him snuggly fur, then choose a ribbon in your favourite colour to tie around his neck!

Materials
100g (3½oz) brown fashion fur yarn (A)
50g (1¾oz) cream DK (8-ply) yarn (B)
Scrap of pink DK (8-ply) yarn for the nose
Two safety eyes
Safety stuffing
Wide satin ribbon

Needles
5.5mm (UK 5, US 9)
3.25mm (UK 10, US 3)

Tension (gauge)
11 sts x 14 rows measures 10 x 10cm (4 x 4in) using 5.5mm (UK 5, US 9) needles over st st

Size
20cm (8in) wide, 30cm (12in) tall

Notes
It is very difficult to count the rows on this yarn so mark them down as you knit them.

Body
Worked in st st.
Using 5.5mm (UK 5, US 9) needles and yarn A cast on 10 sts.

Next row: purl.
Next row: knit increasing in every stitch to end (20 sts).
Beginning with a purl row, work 3 rows in st st.
Next row: * k1, inc in next st, rep from * to end (30 sts).
Beginning with a purl row, work 3 rows in st st.
Next row: * k1, inc in next st, rep from * to end (45 sts).
Beginning with a purl row, work 11 rows in st st.

Shape top
Next row: * k1, k2tog, rep from * to end of row (30 sts).
Beginning with a purl row, work 3 rows in st st.
Next row: (k2tog) across row (15 sts).
Next row: purl.
Break yarn and run through stitches left on needle. Draw up and fasten off.

Head

Worked in st st.

Using 5.5mm (UK 5, US 9) needles and yarn A cast on 10 sts.

Next row: purl.

Next row: knit increasing in every st to end (20 sts).

Beginning with a purl row, work 3 rows in st st.

Next row: * k1, inc in next st, rep from * to end (30 sts).

Beginning with a purl row, work 9 rows in st st.

Shape top of head

Next row: * k1, k2tog, rep from * to end of row (20 sts).

Beginning with a purl row, work 3 rows in st st.

Next row: (k2tog) across row (10 sts).

Next row: purl.

Break yarn and run through stitches left on needle. Draw up and fasten off.

Muzzle

Worked in garter stitch.

Note: muzzle is worked sideways.

Using 3.25mm (UK 10, US 3) needles and yarn B cast on 10 sts.

Work 2 rows in garter stitch.

Inc 1 st at each end of next and foll alt rows to 18 sts.

Work 30 rows in garter stitch.

Dec 1 st at each end of the next and following alt rows to 10 sts.

Work 2 rows in garter stitch and cast off.

Nose

Worked in st st.

Using 3.25mm (UK 10, US 3) needles and pink yarn cast on 8 sts.

Work 6 rows in st st.

Dec 1 st at each end of next and following alt rows to 2 sts.

K2tog and fasten off.

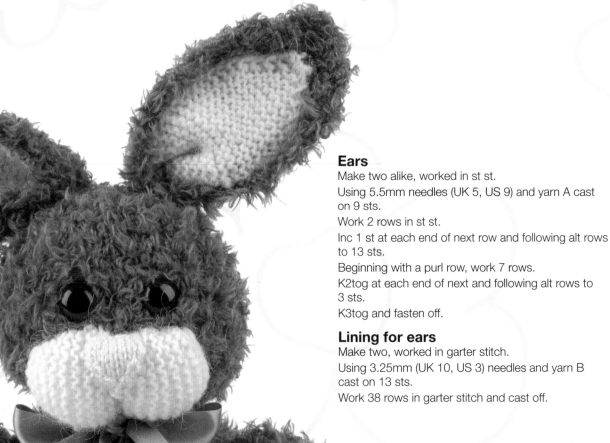

Ears

Make two alike, worked in st st.

Using 5.5mm needles (UK 5, US 9) and yarn A cast on 9 sts.

Work 2 rows in st st.

Inc 1 st at each end of next row and following alt rows to 13 sts.

Beginning with a purl row, work 7 rows.

K2tog at each end of next and following alt rows to 3 sts.

K3tog and fasten off.

Lining for ears

Make two, worked in garter stitch.

Using 3.25mm (UK 10, US 3) needles and yarn B cast on 13 sts.

Work 38 rows in garter stitch and cast off.

the cast-off part of the nose tightly along the centre line of the muzzle, sew back up through the muzzle to the tip of the nose and pull firmly to accentuate the cheeks. Secure. Insert the safety eyes on either side of the head, just above the muzzle. Finish stuffing the head then close the base.

To create each ear, sew together one ear piece and one lining piece. Pleat the base to form the ear shape and sew firmly to the top of the rabbit's head, with one on either side. Sew the body seam and stuff firmly before closing. Now sew the head to the body.

Sew the seams on the arms and feet, leaving an opening. Stuff lightly before closing completely. Flatten the feet out and sew in place on the base of the rabbit. Sew an arm to either side of the body, just below the head. Make a large pompom tail out of yarn B and sew to back of body. Finally, tie the ribbon firmly around the neck of the bunny in a neat bow.

Feet

Make two alike, worked in st st.
Using 5.5mm (UK 5, US 9) needles and yarn A cast on 6 sts.
Next row: purl.
Next row: inc in every st (12 sts).
Next row: purl.
Next row: * k1, inc in next st, rep from * to end (18 sts).
Next row: purl.
Continue in st st until work measures 8cm (3in).
Next row: * k1 k2tog, rep from * to end (12 sts).
Next row: purl.
Next row: (k2tog) across row (6 sts).
Cast off.

Arms

Make two alike, worked in st st.
Using 5.5mm (UK 5, US 9) needles and yarn A cast on 8 sts.
Work in st st for 5cm (2in) ending with a purl row.
Cast off.

Making up

Using a wide-eyed blunt-ended needle, sew the seam on the head, leaving an opening. Stuff firmly and form into a neat ball shape, but do not close. Take the muzzle and pin it in position on the front of the head, about two-thirds of the way down. Stuff the muzzle and then stitch it in place. Puff out the cheeks as you do so. Take the nose and sew it in place in the centre of the muzzle. Pull the yarn from

Little Grey Bunny

This sweet little bunny could be made in any colours you like. In fact, once you have completed the pattern, why not make her a selection of different outfits so that you can change the colour any time you want?

Materials
50g (1¾oz) grey DK (8-ply) yarn (A)
50g (1¾oz) purple DK (8-ply) yarn (B)
Small amounts of cream DK (8-ply) yarn (C)
Small amounts of dark pink DK (8-ply) yarn (D)
Small amounts of dark grey and green DK (8-ply) yarn for embroidery
Safety stuffing
Two small heart beads
Narrow pink ribbon

Needles
3.75mm (UK 9, US 5)

Tension (gauge)
22 sts x 30 rows measures 10 x 10cm (4 x 4in) using 3.75mm (UK 9, US 5) needles over st st

Size
18cm (7in) wide, 25cm (10in) tall

Head
Worked in garter stitch.
Using yarn A and 3.75mm (UK 9, US 5) needles cast on 8 sts.
Knit 2 rows in garter stitch.
Next row: inc in every st to end (16 sts).
Next two rows: knit.
Next row: * k1, inc in next st, rep from * to end (24 sts).
Next two rows: knit.

Next row: k1, * inc in next st, k2, rep from * to last 2 sts, inc in next st, k1 (32 sts).
Work 14 rows straight in garter stitch.
Next row: k1, * k2tog, k2, rep from * to last 3 sts, k2tog, k1 (24 sts).
Next row: knit.
Next row: (k1, k2tog) to end (16 sts).
Next row: knit.
Next row: (k2tog) across row.
Break yarn and run through sts on needle, draw up and fasten off.

Ears
Make two alike, worked in garter stitch.
Using 3.75mm (UK 9, US 5) needles and yarn A cast on 5 sts.
Next row: knit.
Next row: inc 1 st at each end of row (7 sts).
Next row: knit.
Repeat last 2 rows once more (9 sts).
Work 30 rows in garter stitch.
Cast off.

Body
Make back and front alike, worked in garter stitch.
Using 3.75mm (UK 9, US 5) and yarn A cast on 12 sts.
Work 2 rows garter stitch.
Inc 1 st at each end of next and following alt rows until you have 18 sts.
Work 26 rows in garter stitch.

18

Divide for legs

Next row: k8, cast off 2 sts, k to end.

Proceed on first set of sts for leg.

Knit 18 rows.

Next row: k2tog at each end of next row (6 sts).

Next row: knit.

Cast off.

Return to remaining sts and work to match first leg.

Arms

Make two alike, worked in garter stitch.

Using 3.75mm (UK 9, US 5) needles and yarn A cast on 6 sts.

Knit 1 row.

Next row: inc in each st to end (12 sts).

Work 4 rows garter stitch.

Next row: inc 1 st at each end of row (14 sts).

Work 20 rows garter stitch.

Dec 1 st at each end of the next and following alt row (10 sts).

Next row: k2, (k2tog) 3 times, k2 (7 sts).

Knit 1 row and cast off. This is the top of the arm.

Shoes

Make two alike, worked in garter stitch.

Using 3.75mm (UK 9, US 5) needles and yarn B cast on 14 sts.

Knit 1 row.

Next row: inc in each st to end (28 sts).

Work 5 rows in garter stitch.

Next row: k2tog, k8, (k2tog) 4 times, k8, k2tog (22 sts).

Next row: knit.

Next row: k9, (k2tog) twice, k9 (20 sts).

Next row: knit.

Next row: k6, cast off 8 sts, knit to end.

Next row: k6, turn.

Next row: cast on 14 sts, knit to end.

Next row: knit. Cast off.

Return to remaining stitches, rejoin yarn and knit to end.

Work 3 rows in garter stitch and cast off.

Dress

Make back and front alike, worked in st st and garter stitch.

Using 3.75mm (UK 9, US 5) needles and yarn C cast on 24 sts.

Work 4 rows in st st.

Cast off 2 sts at the beg of the next 2 rows (20 sts).

Next row: k2tog at each end of row (18 sts).

Next row: purl.

Work 8 rows in st st. Break C, join in B.

Work 3 rows in garter stitch. Cast off. This is the top of the dress.

Using 3.75mm (UK 9, US 5) needles and yarn B, with right side facing, pick up and knit 24 sts along the cast on edge.

Purl 1 row.

Next row: knit twice into each st to end (48 sts).

Beginning with a purl row, work 15 rows in st st.

Next 2 rows: purl.

Next row: knit.

Next row: purl.

Work 3 rows in garter stitch and cast off.

Sleeves

Make two alike, worked in garter stitch and st st.

Using 3.75mm (UK 9, US 5) needles and yarn B cast on 24 sts.

Next 2 rows: knit.

Beginning with a purl row, work 3 rows in st st.

Next row: purl.

Next row: purl.

Next row: knit.

Next row: purl.

Beginning with a knit row, work 6 rows in st st.

Cast off.

Bow

Worked in garter stitch.

Using 3.75mm (UK 9, US 5) needles and yarn D cast on 5 sts.

Work 44 rows in garter stitch. Cast off.

Making up

Partly sew the seam on the head, then stuff and shape it before closing completely. Take the ears and pleat them at the base to give them shape. Sew to either side of the head. Embroider the eyes and nose with dark grey DK (8-ply) yarn.

Sew the side seams of the body and legs, leaving the neck edge open for stuffing. Stuff the rabbit firmly then close. Partly sew the seams on the arms and then stuff. Close them completely then sew one to each side of the body at shoulder level. Sew the head to the body securely.

Take the shoes and sew the foot and back seam. Insert a tiny bit of stuffing into the toe part to give it shape, place the base of the leg inside the shoe and stitch the shoe in place. Reverse the seams on one shoe so that strap will come on the opposite side of the foot. Sew beads on as buttons, or embroider a French knot instead.

To make up the dress, work in all the ends. Put the pieces together with the right sides facing inwards and catch the bodice together at each side. Sew the sleeves in place along the armholes, easing if needed. Next join the side and sleeve seams. Turn right side out. Embroider a flower onto the front of the dress bodice using dark green and dark pink yarn. Slip onto the rabbit and secure the shoulder seams to each side of the neck. Thread a piece of narrow ribbon through the fabric at the waistline and tie in a bow at the front of the dress.

Sew the short end of the bow, then fold in half with the seam at the centre back. Gather the centre of the piece together to form a bow. Sew to the top of the head.

Finger Puppets

Children will love these cute little finger puppets. They require only a very small amount of yarn and can be knitted in just a couple of hours. Use my colour choices or choose from similar weight yarns in your stash. Stripe them or use single colours – it's fast and easy to create your own family of tiny bunnies.

Materials

Small amounts of 4-ply (fingering) yarn in colours of your choice
Tiny buttons
Small amount of stuffing

Needles

3.25mm (UK 10, US 3)

Tension (gauge)

The tension (gauge) is not critical for this project

Size

2.5cm (1in) wide, 6cm (2½in) tall

Base

Worked in garter stitch, then st st.
Using 3.25mm (UK 10, US 3) needles and colour of your choice cast on 20 sts.
Rows 1–3: work in garter stitch.
Rows 4–20: beginning with a knit row, work in st st.

Shape top

Row 21: * k2, k2tog, rep from * to end (15 sts).
Row 22: purl.
Row 23: * k1, k2tog, rep from * to end (10 sts).
Row 24: purl.

Row 25: (k2tog) across row (5 sts).
Break yarn and run through sts on needle, draw up and fasten off.

Head

Worked in st st.
Using 3.25mm (UK 10, US 3) needles and appropriate coloured yarn cast on 4 sts.
Row 1: purl.
Row 2: inc in each st to end (8 sts).
Row 3: purl.
Row 4: * k1, inc in next st, rep from * to end (12 sts).
Row 5: purl.
Repeat last 2 rows (18 sts).
Rows 8–9: beginning with a knit row, work in st st.
Row 10: * k1, k2tog, rep from * to end (12 sts).
Row 11: purl.
Row 12: * k1, k2tog, rep from * to end (8 sts).
Break yarn and run through sts, draw up and fasten off.

Ears

Make two alike, worked in garter stitch.

Using appropriate colour and 3.25mm (UK 10, US 3) needles cast on 3 sts.

Row 1: knit

Row 2: inc in first and last st (5 sts).

Row 3: knit.

Rows 4–8: work in garter stitch.

Row 9: k2tog at each end of row (3 sts).

Row 10: knit.

Row 11: k3tog, and fasten off.

Bow

Worked in garter stitch.

Using appropriate yarn and 3.25mm (UK 10, US 3) needles cast on 10 sts.

Rows 1–3: work in garter stitch.

Cast off.

Making up

Sew the seam of the head, leaving a small opening for stuffing. Stuff quite firmly then sew up the opening. Using the photographs as a guide, embroider eyes and a nose using dark 4-ply (fingering) yarn.

Catch each ear together at the cast-on edge to form a tiny pleat. Sew the ears to the top of the head, either sticking up or angled downwards to form lop ears. Sew the side seam of the base then attach the head to the top of the base piece.

Take the bow and run a thread through the centre line of the knitting, gathering it up tightly to form a bow shape. Sew to the centre of head, between the ears. Attach colourful buttons to the front of the base.

What do bunnies sing at birthday parties?

Hoppy birthday to you!

Stripy Bunny

The cute, cuddly character is fun and easy to make. I created the eyes from felt and attached them at the end, but you could easily adapt the design and use safety or embroidered eyes to complete your rabbit.

Materials
50g (1¾oz) DK (8-ply) yarn in variegated greens, blues and and oranges (A)
Small amounts of lime green DK (8-ply) yarn (B)
Small amounts of black and white DK (8-ply) yarn
Safety stuffing
Small pieces of black and white felt for eyes

Needles
4.5mm (UK 7, US 7)
4.0mm (UK 8, US 6)

Tension (gauge)
20 sts x 28 rows measures 10 x 10cm (4 x 4in) using 4.5mm (UK 7, US 7) needles over garter stitch

Size
27cm (10¾in) wide, 22cm (8¾in) tall

Notes
Rabbit is worked entirely in garter stitch, apart from the teeth.

Rabbit
Front and back alike.
Using yarn A and 4.5mm (UK 7, US 7) needles cast on 7 sts.
Row 1: knit.
Row 2: inc in each st across row (14 sts).
Row 3: knit.
Row 4: inc in each st across row (28 sts).
Row 5: knit.
Rows 6–40: work in garter stitch.
Row 41: k2tog at each end of the row (26 sts).
Row 42: knit.
Rep last 2 rows once more (24 sts).
Row 45: k10, cast off 4 sts, k to end.
Work on first set of 10 sts for first ear:
Rows 1–20: knit.
Row 21: k2tog at each end of row (8 sts).
Row 22: knit.
Rep last 2 rows until you have 2 sts remaining, k2tog and fasten off.
Return to remaining 10 sts and work to match first ear.

Muzzle
Using yarn B and 4.0mm (UK 8, US 6) needles cast on 24 sts.
Work 8 rows in garter stitch.

Divide work
Next row: k12, turn and work on these sts for first side.
Next row: k2tog at each end of row (10 sts).
Next row: knit.
Rep last 2 rows until you have 4 sts, cast off.
Return to remaining stitches and work to match first half.

Nose

Using black yarn and 4.0mm (UK 8, US 6) needles cast on 8 sts.

Knit 4 rows in garter stitch.

Next row: k2tog at each end of row (6 sts).

Next row: knit.

Rep last 2 rows once more (4 sts).

Next row: (k2tog) twice (2 sts).

Next row: k2tog and fasten off.

Teeth

Make two alike, worked in st st.

Using 4.0mm (UK 8, US 6) needles and white yarn cast on 4 sts.

Work 8 rows in st st. Cast off.

These teeth were made for munching!

Arms and feet

Make four alike.

Using 4.0mm (UK 8, US 6) needles and yarn B cast on 8 sts.

Next row: knit.

Next row: inc in each st across the row (16 sts).

Next row: knit.

Next row: * k1, inc in next st, rep from * to end (24 sts).

Next row: knit.

Continue in garter stitch (every row knit) for a further 8 rows.

Next row: * k1, skpo, rep from * to end (16 sts).

Work 12 rows in garter stitch.

Next row: * k1, skpo, rep from * to the last st, k1 (11 sts).

Next row: knit.

Next row: k1, * k2tog, rep from * to end (6 sts).

Break yarn and run through sts on needle, draw up tight and fasten off.

Making up

Sew the back and the front of the rabbit together, leaving the base unsewn. Stuff the body and sew up the base to close completely. Using matching yarn, gather the base of each ear together to give it shape then stitch to the top of the head.

Pin the muzzle in place on the front of the face, insert a small amount of stuffing behind it, then stitch in position. Stitch the nose in place in the centre. Fold the teeth in half and stitch the side seams. Sew to the centre of the muzzle at the base, using the photographs as a guide. Embroider the whiskers with black DK (8-ply) yarn.

Cut felt shapes for the eyes, and glue or sew in place. Partly sew the seams of the arms and legs, then stuff, but not too firmly, before sewing closed. Sew the arms on either side of body. Flatten the leg pieces then stitch in place on base. Try to get them level so the rabbit will stand upright.

Make a pompom from white DK (8-ply) yarn and attach it to the body.

Jelly Bunnies

Here is a pattern designed for the novice knitter or for children who have just learned to knit. These cute little bunnies with expressions to match your mood are so quick and simple to knit. They have very little sewing up to do and can be made in just a couple of evenings.

Materials
50g (1¾oz) neon pink, green and yellow DK (8-ply) yarn
Safety stuffing
Embroidery cotton for features
Butterfly motifs if desired

Needles
4.0mm (UK 8, US 6)
3.25mm (UK 10, US 3)

Tension (gauge)
22 sts x 30 rows measures 10 x 10cm (4 x 4in) using 4.0mm (UK 8, US 6) needles over st st

Size
12cm (4¾in) wide, 18cm (7in) tall

Body, head and legs
Using 4.0mm (UK 8, US 6) needles and colour of your choice cast on 30 sts.
Rows 1–4: work in garter stitch.
Rows 5–40: beginning with a knit row, work in st st.

Shape top of head
Row 1: * k3, k2tog, rep from * to end (24 sts).
Row 2: purl.
Row 3: * k2, k2tog, rep from * to end (18 sts).
Row 4: purl.
Row 5: * k1, k2tog, rep from * to end (12 sts).
Row 6: (p2tog) across row (6 sts).
Break yarn and run through sts on needle, draw up tight and fasten off.

Arms
Make two, worked in st st.
Using 4.0mm (UK 8, US 6) needles and colour of your choice cast on 4 sts.
Row 1: purl.
Row 2: inc in every st to end (8 sts).
Row 3: purl.
Row 4: inc every st to end (16 sts).
Rows 5–15: beginning with a purl row, work in st st.

Row 16: (k2tog) across row (8 sts).
Row 17: purl.
Row 18: (k2tog) across row (4 sts).
Break yarn and run thread through sts on needle, draw thread through and secure.

Ears
Make two alike, worked in garter stitch.
Using 3.25mm (UK 10, US 3) needles and colour of your choice cast on 4 sts.
Row 1: knit.
Row 2: inc in first and last st (6 sts).
Row 3: knit.
Rep last 2 rows to 10 sts.
Rows 8–23: work in garter stitch.
This is the base of the ear.
Cast off.

Making up
Partly sew up the head and body piece along the seam. This will run down the back of the bunny. Stuff quite firmly, then sew closed. Count 14 rows down from the first row of head shaping, and mark this row for the neckline. Take a blunt-ended needle and thread it with matching yarn. Secure the yarn to the back seam at the marked row. Now run the yarn through each stitch all around the neckline to the back seam where you began. Pull the yarn firmly and you will see the head begin to take shape. Continue pulling until the head forms a nice rounded ball shape. Don't over-tighten. Secure the yarn at the back seam.

To define the legs, begin at the centre base of the rabbit. You will now sew through the whole thickness of the body from back to front. Sew backwards and forwards, drawing the stitches tight as you do. Continue working along the first 12 rows then secure the thread and fasten off.

Take the ears and make a pleat at the base of each one by folding each side into the centre and catching together with a few stitches. Sew the ears to the top of the bunny's head. Make a small pompom from matching yarn and attach it to the body. Embroider the facial features with dark yarn of your choice. Attach a butterfly motif, or similar, if desired.

Egg Cosies

These cute egg cosies are so quick to make, and take just a small amount of DK (8-ply) yarn. It's an ideal way to use yarns from your stash. I have not stated colours, so follow my choices or make your own unique versions.

Materials

Small amounts of DK (8-ply) yarn in four colours per cosy
Small amount of safety stuffing
Small ribbon bow (optional)

Needles

3.75mm (UK 9, US 5)

Tension (gauge)

The tension (gauge) is not critical for this project

Size

Diameter 6cm (2½in) – will fit an average-sized egg – 12cm (4¾in) tall

Boy Cosy

Using 3.75mm (UK 9, US 5) cast on 30 sts in colour A.
Work 3 rows garter stitch.
Change to st st and join in colour B.
Work in stripes of 2 rows B and 2 rows A for 12 rows.
Break yarn B.

Shape top

Next row: * k2, k2tog, rep from * to last 2 sts, k2 (23 sts).
Next row: purl.
Next row: * k1, k2tog, rep from * to last 2 sts, k2 (16 sts).
Next row: purl.
Break A and join in C.
Proceed for head.
Work 8 rows in st st.

Shape top of head

Next row: * k2, k2tog, rep from * to end (12 sts).
Next row: purl.
Next row: * k1, k2tog, rep from * to end (8 sts).
Next row: purl.
Next row: (k2tog) across row (4 sts).
Break yarn and thread through rem sts, draw up and fasten off.

Ears

Make two alike, worked in garter stitch.

Using 3.75mm (UK 9, US 5) needles and colour C cast on 2 sts.

Knit 1 row.

Next row: inc in first st, k1 (3 sts).

Next row: knit.

Next row: inc in first and last st (5 sts).

Work 6 rows in garter stitch.

Next row: k2tog at each end of row (3 sts).

Knit 3 rows. Cast off. This is base of the ear.

Neckerchief

Worked in garter stitch.

Using 3.75mm (UK 9, US 5) needles and colour D cast on 2 sts.

Next row: knit.

Next row: inc in each st (4 sts).

Next row: knit.

Inc 1 st at each end of next and following alt rows to 12 sts.

Next 2 rows: knit.

Divide for ties

Next row: k3, cast off 6 sts, k to end.

Work on 3 sts for ties.

Knit 14 rows.

Next row: k2tog, k1 (2 sts).

Next row: k2tog. Fasten off.

Work other side to match.

Girl Cosy

Using 3.75mm (UK 9, US 5) cast on 30 sts in colour A.

Work 3 rows garter stitch.

Change to st st and join in colour B.

Work 2 rows in st st in B.

Next row: using A, k2, sl1, * k3, sl1, rep from * to last 3 sts, k3.

Next row: using A, p3, sl1 purlwise, rep from * to last 2 sts, p2.

Work 2 rows in st st in colour B.

Next row: using A, k4, * sl1, k3, rep from * to last 2 sts, sl1, k1.

Next row: using A, p1, sl1 purlwise, * p3, sl1, rep from * to last 4 sts, p4.

Work 2 rows in colour B.

Next row: using A, k2, sl1, * k3, sl1, rep from * to last 3 sts, k3.

Next row: using A, * p3, sl1 purlwise, rep from * to last 2 sts, p2.

Break A and continue in B.

Shape top

Next row: *k2, k2tog, rep from * to last 2 sts, k2 (23 sts).

Next row: purl.

Next row: * k1, k2tog, rep from * to last 2 sts, k2 (16 sts).

Next row: purl.

Break colour B and join in colour C.

Proceed for head.

Work 8 rows in st st.

Shape top of head

Next row: * k2, k2tog, rep from * to end (12 sts).
Next row: purl.
Next row: * k1, k2tog, rep from * to end (8 sts).
Next row: purl.
Next row: (k2tog) across row (4 sts).
Break yarn and thread through rem sts, draw up
and fasten off.

Ears

As for the Boy Cosy.

Making up

Work in the ends and sew up the back seam. Stuff
the head section, then take a needle threaded with
matching yarn and run a gathering stitch all around
where the body section ends and the head section
begins. Draw up firmly to form the head. Secure.

Take the ears and pleat the base of each. Sew to
the top of the head. Embroider the facial features
using DK (8-ply) yarn in a colour of your choice. To
complete the boy bunny, embroider white French
knots all over the neckerchief then tie around his
neck. For the girl bunny, sew a ribbon bow to the
front of her dress at her neck.

Glove Puppet

Using just a small amount of yarn you can create this little Christmas glove puppet in only one evening. He will look cute sitting in the top of a Christmas stocking, or simply give him as a gift.

Materials

50g (1¾oz) red DK (8-ply) yarn (A)
50g (1¾oz) green DK (8-ply) yarn (B)
Small amount of beige DK (8-ply) yarn (C)
Small amount of dark brown DK (8-ply) yarn
    for embroidery
Safety stuffing
Tiny bell for hat
Gold beads
Christmas motif (optional)

Needles

3.75mm (UK 9, US 5)

Tension (gauge)

20 sts x 30 rows measures 10 x 10cm (4 x 4in)
    using 3.75mm (UK 9, US 5) needles over st st.

Size

27cm (10½in) wide, 28cm (11in) tall

Head

Worked in st st.
Using 3.75mm (UK 9, US 5) needles and yarn C cast on 10 sts.
Purl 1 row.
Next row: inc in each st to end (20 sts).
Beginning with a purl row, work 3 rows in st st.
Next row: * k1, inc in next st, rep from * to end (30 sts).
Beginning with a purl row, work 9 rows in st st.

Shape top of head

Next row: * k3, k2tog, rep from * to end (24 sts).
Next row: purl.
Next row: * k2, k2tog, rep from * to end (18 sts).
Next row: purl.
Next row: * k1, k2tog, rep from * to end (12 sts).
Next row: purl.
Next row: (k2tog) across row (6 sts).
Break yarn and run through stitches on needle, draw up tight and fasten off.

Ear

Worked in garter stitch.
Using 3.75mm (UK 9, US 5) needles and yarn C cast on 3 sts.
Knit 1 row.
Now inc 1 st at each end of the next and following alt rows to 9 sts.
Work 12 rows garter stitch.
Now dec 1 st at each end of next and following alt rows to 3 sts.
K3tog and fasten off.

Hat

Using 3.75mm (UK 9, US 5) needles and yarn B cast on 36 sts.
Knit 5 rows. Break yarn B and join in yarn A.
Work in st st for 6 rows.

Shape top of hat

Next row: * k4, k2tog, rep from * to end (30 sts).
Next row: purl.
Next row: k4, * k2tog, k3, rep from * to last 6 sts, k2tog, k4 (25 sts).
Next row: purl.
Next row: k4, * k2tog, k2, rep from * to last 5 sts, k2tog, k3 (20 sts).
Next row: purl.
Next row: k4, * k2tog, k1, rep from * to last 4 sts, k2tog, k2 (15 sts).
Next row: purl.
Next row: k4, (k2tog) across row to last st, k1 (10 sts).
Beginning with a purl row, work 7 rows in st st.
Next row: (k2tog) across row (5 sts).
Beginning with a purl row, work 3 rows in st st.
Next row: k2tog, k1, k2tog (3 sts).
Next row: k3tog.

Glove

Make back and front alike.
Using 3.75mm (UK 9, US 5) needles and yarn B cast on 32 sts.
Knit 5 rows.
Change to yarn A.
Work 26 rows in st st.
Cast on 10 sts at the beg of the next 2 rows (52 sts).
Work 14 rows in st st.
Cast off 10 sts at the beg of the next 2 rows (32 sts).
Cast off 3 sts at the beg of the next 6 rows (14 sts).
Cast off 2 sts at the beg of the next 2 rows (10 sts).
Work 4 rows in st st.
Cast off. This is the neck edge. Make another piece to match.
Stitch together the back and front part of the glove along the top of the arms and neck edge.
Now proceed to pick up along each sleeve edge for cuff and paws.
Using 3.75mm (UK 9, US 5) needles and yarn B, with right side facing pick up and knit 24 sts evenly along one sleeve edge.

Work 3 rows in garter stitch, break green and join in yarn C.

Work 2 rows garter stitch.

Dec 1 st each end of every row until 12 sts remain. (K2tog) across row (6 sts).

Cast off.

Work other sleeve edge and paw to match.

Collar

Worked in garter stitch.

Using 3.75mm (UK 9, US 5) needles and yarn B cast on 2 sts and knit one row.

Row 1: inc in each st (4 sts).

Row 2: knit.

Row 3: inc in first st, knit to last st, inc (6 sts).

Repeat rows 2 and 3 until you have 12 sts on the needle. Do not cast off, slip the stitches onto a spare needle. Repeat this process until you have 5 points on your needle, now work across all 60 sts.

Knit 1 row.

Next row: * k2, k2tog, rep from * to end (45 sts).

Next row: knit.

Next row: *k1, k2tog, rep from * to end (30 sts).

Next row: knit.

Cast off.

Making up

Partly sew the head seam, which runs down the back of the head, then stuff firmly but do not close the base. Embroider eyes and a nose onto the face with brown DK (8-ply) yarn. Pleat the base of the ear and sew to one side of the head.

Sew the glove seam. Put a small amount of stuffing in the end of each paw, then sew along the cuff line on each paw to hold the stuffing in place. Attach the glove to the head by pushing the neck part up inside the head a little way and sewing the head in place. Attach the collar and sew the seam at the back of the neck.

Sew the side seam of the hat, then turn right side out. Attach the bell firmly to the point of the hat. Position the hat on one side of the head and sew in place. Sew gold beads to the points all around the collar. Glue or stitch the motif to the front of the glove.

Garden Bunny

This friendly bunny is all ready for work with his overalls, complete with carrot motif. He is made mostly in stocking stitch and his overalls and shirt are an integral part of his body, so he is quite simple to knit.

Materials

50g (1¾oz) blue DK (8-ply) yarn (A)
50g (1¾oz) white DK (8-ply) yarn (B)
50g (1¾oz) cream DK (8-ply) yarn (C)
Small amount of denim blue and dark grey DK (8-ply) yarn
Small amounts of bright green and orange 4-ply (fingering) yarn
Safety stuffing

Needles

4.0mm (UK 8, US 6)
3.25mm (UK 10, US 3)

Tension (gauge)

24 sts x 32 rows measures 10 x 10cm (4 x 4in) using 4.0mm (UK 8, US 6) needles over st st

Size

18cm (7in) wide, 39cm (15½in) tall

Head

Worked in st st.
Using 4.0mm (UK 8, US 6) needles and yarn C cast on 10 sts.
Purl 1 row.
Next row: inc in each st to end (20 sts).
Beginning with a purl row, work 3 rows in st st.
Next row: * k1, inc in next st, rep from * to end (30 sts).
Beginning with a purl row, work 9 rows in st st.

Shape top of head

Next row: * k3, k2tog, rep from * to end (24 sts).
Next row: purl.
Next row: * k2, k2tog, rep from * to end (18 sts).
Next row: purl.
Next row: * k1, k2tog, rep from * to end (12 sts).
Next row: purl.
Next row: (k2tog) across row (6 sts).
Break yarn and run through stitches on needle, draw up tight and fasten off.

Ears

Make two alike, worked in garter stitch.
Using 4.0mm (UK 8, US 6) needles and yarn C cast on 3 sts.
Knit 1 row.
Inc 1 st at each end of the next and following alt rows to 9 sts.
Work 12 rows garter stitch.
Dec 1 st at each end of next and following alt rows to 3 sts.
K3tog and fasten off.

Body and legs

Make two pieces alike.
Using 4.0mm (UK 8, US 6) needles and yarn A cast on 10 sts.
Work 3 rows garter stitch.
Change to st st and work 24 rows.
Leave on stitch holder.
Work another leg to match.

Join legs together

Knit across first set of sts, cast on 1 st, knit across second set of sts (21 sts).

Next row: purl.

Work 14 rows in st st.

Change to garter stitch and work 4 rows.

Break yarn A and join in yarn B.

Work 18 rows in st st.

Dec 1 st at each end of next and following alt rows to 17 sts.

Cast off.

Work another piece the same.

Sleeves and arms

Make two alike, worked in st st and garter stitch.

Using 4.0mm (UK 8, US 6) needles and yarn B cast on 8 sts.

Work 2 rows in st st.

Inc 1 st at each end of next and every following row until you have 18 sts.

Next row: purl.

Work 6 rows in st st.

Change to garter stitch and work 4 rows.

Break yarn B and change to yarn C.

Work in st st for 14 rows.

Next row: * k1, inc in next st, rep from * to end (27 sts).

Work 6 rows.

Shape top

Next row: k1, (k2tog) across row (14 sts).

Next row: purl.

Next row: (k2tog) across row (7 sts).

Next row: purl.

Next row: (k2tog) 3 times. K1 (4 sts).

Break yarn and run through sts.

Draw up and fasten off.

Feet

Make two alike, worked in st st.

Using 4.0mm (UK 8, US 6) needles and yarn C cast on 24 sts.

Work 6 rows in st st.

Next row: k8, inc in each of next 8 sts, k8 (32 sts).

Beginning with a purl row, work 3 rows in st st.

Next row: k14, inc in each of next 4 sts, k14 (36 sts).

Beginning with a purl row, work 3 rows in st st.

Next row: (k2tog) across row (18 sts).

Next row: purl.

Next row: (k2tog) across row (9 sts).

Run thread through sts, draw up and fasten off.

Bib

Using 4.0mm (UK 8, US 6) needles and yarn A cast on 18 sts.

Knit 2 rows.

Next row: knit.

Next row: k2, purl to last 2 sts, k2.

Repeat last 2 rows 4 times more.

Work 4 rows garter stitch.

Carrot top
Using 3.25mm (UK 10, US 3) needles and green 4-ply (fingering) yarn cast on 20 sts and then cast off.

Making up
With right sides facing, sew the body pieces together leaving the neck edge and base of legs open. Turn right sides out. Stuff firmly, then close the neck edge.

Sew the arm seams, leaving the tops open, then stuff fairly firmly. Sew to the body at shoulder height on each side. Sew the back seam of the feet then stuff firmly. Insert the feet inside the base of the legs and sew in place. Sew the patch to one of the bunny's trouser legs.

Sew the head seam, leaving the base open, then stuff firmly and close the base. Sew an ear to either side of the head, pleating at the base to create a soft, shape. Embroider the facial features using dark grey DK (8-ply) yarn. Sew the head to the body.

Take the bib and sew the tiny carrot onto the front of it. Coil the green to resemble leaves and sew in place. Sew the bib to the front of the overalls at the waist. Take the straps over the shoulders, cross them at the back, then sew to the waist of the overalls.

Next row: k4, cast off 10 sts, k to end.
Work on first set of 4 sts for strap.
Work 36 rows in garter stitch and cast off.
Return to remaining 4 sts and complete to match.

Patch
Using 4.0mm (UK 8, US 6) needles and denim blue cast on 10 sts.
Work 12 rows garter stitch. Cast off.

Carrot
Worked in st st.
Using orange 4-ply (fingering) yarn and 3.25mm (UK 10, US 3) needles cast on 1 st.
Next row: inc in first st (2 sts).
Next row: purl.
Next row: inc in each st (4 sts).
Next row: purl.
Next row: inc in first and last st (6 sts).
Next row: purl.
Work 4 rows in st st and cast off.

Yum... tasty and nutritious!

Bunny with Carrot

Every bunny needs a juicy carrot for lunch and this bunny is no exception. He is made in luxury baby alpaca yarn to give him a furry coat as soft as silk. You can substitute the yarn for any DK (8-ply) weight as long as you work to a similar tension (gauge).

Materials

50g (1¾oz) brown alpaca DK (8-ply) yarn (A)
50g (1¾oz) cream alpaca DK (8-ply) yarn (B)
Small amounts of orange and green DK (8-ply) yarn to make the carrot
Small amount of dark grey DK (8-ply) yarn for the rabbit's facial features
Safety stuffing

Needles

4.0mm (UK 8, US 6)

Tension (gauge)

22 sts x 30 rows measures 10 x 10cm (4 x 4in) using 4.0mm (UK 8, US 6) needles over st st

Size

12cm (4¾in) wide, 22cm (8¾in) high when sitting; carrot 14cm (5½in) long

Head

Worked in st st.
Using 4.0mm (UK 8, US 6) needles and yarn A cast on 10 sts.
Purl 1 row.
Next row: inc in each st to end (20 sts).
Beginning with a purl row, work 3 rows in st st.
Next row: * k1, inc, rep from * to end (30 sts).
Beginning with a purl row, work 5 rows in st st.
Next row: * k2, inc, rep from * to end (40 sts).

Beginning with a purl row, work 7 rows.
Next row: * k2, skpo, rep from * to end (30 sts).
Beginning with a purl row, work 3 rows in st st.
Next row: * k1, skpo, rep from * to end (20 sts).
Change to yarn B.
Beginning with a purl row, work 3 rows in st st.
Next row: (k2tog) across row (10 sts).
Next row: purl.
Next row: (k2tog) 5 times, break yarn and run through sts on needle, draw up and fasten off. This is the nose end of the piece.

Ears

Make two alike, worked entirely in garter stitch.
Using 4.0mm (UK 8, US 6) needles and yarn A cast on 5 sts.
Knit 2 rows.
Inc 1 st each end of next and following alt rows to 15 sts.
Work 37 rows in garter stitch.
Next row: k2tog at each end of row (13 sts).
Next row: knit.
Rep last 2 rows until you have 9 sts.
Work 1 row and cast off. This is the top of the ear.

Body

Worked in st st.

Using 4.0mm (UK 8, US 6) needles and yarn A cast on 10 sts.

Purl 1 row.

Next row: inc in each st to end (20 sts).

Beginning with a purl row, work 3 rows in st st.

Next row: * k1, inc, rep from * to end (30 sts).

Beginning with a purl row, work 3 rows in st st.

Next row: * k2, inc, rep from * to end (40 sts).

Beginning with a purl row, work 3 rows in st st.

Next row: * k3, inc, rep from * to end (50 sts).

Beginning with a purl row, work 11 rows.

Next row: * k3, skpo, rep from * to end (40 sts).

Beginning with a purl row, work 3 rows in st st.

Now work the front bib. You will need to join in separate balls of brown and cream and twist the yarns at the back of the work when changing colour to avoid holes.

Next row: k17 A, k6 B, k17 A.

Next row: p16 A, p8 B, p16 A.

Next row: k15 A, k10 B, k15 A.

Next row: p14 A, p12 B, p14 A.

Next row: k13 A, k14 B, k13 A.

Next row: p12 A, p16 B, p12 A.

Next row: k12 A, k16 B, k12 A.

Next row: p12 A, p16 B, p12 A.

Repeat last 2 rows 4 times more.

Next row: keeping bib pattern correct * k2, skpo, rep from * to end (30 sts).

Next row: p9 in A to bib, p12 B across bib, purl in A to end.

Next row: k11 A, k8 B, k11 A.

Next row: k12 A, k6 B, k12 A.

Break B and spare ball A.

Continue in A only.

Next row: purl.

Next row: * k1, skpo, rep from * to end (20 sts).

Next row: purl.

Next row: (k2tog) across row, break yarn and run through sts on needle, draw up and fasten off.

Legs

Make two alike, worked in st st.

Using needles size 4.0mm (UK 8, US 6) and yarn A cast on 10 sts.

Purl 1 row.

Next row: inc in each st to end (20 sts).

Next row: k1, inc in each of the next 18 sts, k1 (38 sts).

Beginning with a purl row, work 11 rows in st st.

Shape the foot

Next row: k9, (k2tog) 10 times, k9 (28 sts).

Next row: purl.

Next row: k9, (k2tog) 5 times, k9 (23 sts).

Beginning with a purl row, work 3 rows in st st.

Next row: k10, sl1, k2tog, psso, k10 (21 sts).

Beginning with a purl row, work 19 rows in st st.

Next row: (k2tog) to last st, k1 (11 sts).

Next row: purl.

Next row: (k2tog) across row, break yarn and run through sts on needle, draw up and fasten off.

Beginning with a purl row, work 9 rows.
Next row: * k4, skpo, rep from * to end (25 sts).
Next row: purl.
Next row: * k3, skpo, rep from * to end (20 sts).
Next row: purl.
Next row: * k2, skpo, rep from * to end (15 sts).
Beginning with a purl row, work 3 rows.
Next row: * k1, skpo, rep from * to end (10 sts).
Beginning with a purl row, work 3 rows.
Next row: (k2tog) across row (5 sts).
Beginning with a purl row, work 5 rows.
Next row: (k2tog) twice, k1 (3 sts).
Next row: p3tog, fasten off.

Leaves
Using 4.0mm (UK 8, US 6) needles and green cast
50 sts. Cast off.

Making up
Begin with the head. Weave in the ends and partly
sew the seam, which will run underneath the head.
Stuff firmly before closing. Gently pleat the ears at the
base then stitch to either side of the head. Embroider
the facial features with dark grey DK (8-ply) yarn.

Sew the body seam, which runs down the centre
of the rabbit's back. Stuff firmly and then close.
Partly sew the seams on the arms and legs, stuffing
each piece before closing; add extra to the feet to
give them a nice shape. Sew the arms and legs to
the body. Remember to position the legs in a sitting
position. Sew the head firmly to the body, tilting it
slightly to one side to give a cute appearance. Make a
pompom from yarn B and attach to the body.

Take the carrot and partly sew the side seam. Stuff
firmly before closing. Fold the leaf section into loops
to resemble leaves. Sew to the top of the carrot.
Catch the arms of the rabbit together at the bottom
and then place the carrot into the bunny's arms.

Arms
Make two alike, worked in st st.
Using 4.0mm (UK 8, US 6) needles and yarn A cast
on 10 sts.
Purl 1 row.
Next row: k1, inc in each st to last st, k1 (18 sts).
Beginning with a purl row, work 3 rows in st st.
Next row: k1, * inc, k2, rep from * to last 2 sts, inc,
k1 (24 sts).
Beginning with a purl row, work 25 rows in st st.
Next row: k1, * skpo, k2, rep from * to last 3 sts, k3
(19 sts).
Beginning with a purl row, work 3 rows in st st.
Next row: k1, * inc, k1, rep from * to last 2 sts, k2
(27 sts).
Beginning with a purl row, work 7 rows in st st.
Next row: k2tog, * skpo, rep from * to last 3 sts, k1,
k2tog (16 sts).
Purl.
Next row: (k2tog) across row. Cast off.

Carrot
Worked in st st.
Using 4.0mm (UK 8, US 6) and orange yarn cast
on 10 sts.
Purl.
Next row: inc in every st to end (20 sts).
Next row: purl.
Next row: * k1, inc, rep from * to end (30 sts).

Fairy Bunny

Every little girl will just love to own this special fairy bunny, complete with flower petal dress, rose hairpiece and necklace, and tiny shoes to match. Use my colour choices or select your own shades.

Materials

50g (1¾oz) sparkly white DK (8-ply) yarn (A)
50g (1¾oz) pale pink DK (8-ply) yarn (B)
50g (1¾oz) pistachio green DK (8-ply) yarn (C)
Small amount of black DK (8-ply) yarn for the rabbit's face
Small amount of pink ribbon
Ribbon rose
Safety stuffing

Needles

4.0mm (UK 8, US 6)

Tension (gauge)

22 sts x 30 rows measures 10 x 10cm (4 x 4in) using size 4.0mm (UK 8, US 6) needles over st st

Size

17cm (6½in) wide, 39cm (15½in) tall

Body and head made in one piece

Worked in st st.
Using 4.0mm (UK 8, US 6) needles and yarn A cast on 10 sts.
Purl 1 row.
Next row: inc in each st to end (20 sts).
Beginning with a purl row, work 3 rows in st st.
Next row: * k1, inc, rep from * to end (30 sts).
Beginning with a purl row, work 3 rows in st st.
Next row: * k2, inc, rep from * to end (40 sts).

Beginning with a purl row, work 3 rows in st st.
Next row: * k3, inc, rep from * to end (50 sts).
Beginning with a purl row, work 29 rows.
Mark row for neck.
Work 22 rows in st st.

Shape head

Next row: * k3, skpo, rep from * to end (40 sts).
Next row: purl.
Next row: * k2, skpo, rep from * to end (30 sts).
Next row: purl.
Next row: * k1, skpo, rep from * to end (20 sts).
Next row: purl.
Next row: (k2tog) across row (10 sts).
Break yarn and run through sts on needle, draw up and fasten off.

Arms

Make two alike, worked in st st.
Using A and 4.0mm (UK 8, US 6) needles cast on 9 sts (this is the top of the arm).
Purl 1 row.
Next row: inc in each st to end (18 sts).
Beginning with a purl row, work in st st for a further 19 rows.
Next row: * k2, inc in next st, rep from * to end (24 sts).
Next row: purl.
Work 6 rows in st st.
Next row: (k2tog) across row (12 sts).
Next row: purl.
Next row: (k2tog) across row (6 sts).
Break yarn and run through sts on needle, draw up and fasten off.

Ears

Make two alike, worked in st st.
Using 4.0mm (UK 8, US 6) needles and shade A cast on 18 sts.
Work 16 rows in st st.
Next row: k4, skpo, k6, k2tog, k4 (16 sts).
Next row: purl.
Next row: k2tog, k2, skpo, k4, k2tog, k2, skpo (12 sts).
Next row: purl.
Next row: k2tog, k1, skpo, k2, k2tog, k1, skpo (8 sts).
Next row: purl.
Next row: k2tog, skpo, k2tog, skpo (4 sts).
Cast off.

Making up the rabbit

Sew the seam on the head and body leaving the base open to stuff. Push stuffing into the head section first, making it quite firm and round. Take a needle and yarn and starting at the seam on the marked row for the neck, weave the yarn in and out of the stitches all around. Pull firmly to create a nice rounded shape for the head. Secure very firmly at the back seam. Stuff the rest of the body firmly then close the base.

Fold each ear in half, then sew the seam for each – this runs down the back of the ear. Sew an ear to each side of the head. Pleat at the base to give fullness and shape. Embroider the eyes, nose and mouth using black DK (8-ply) yarn. Partly sew the arm seams, stuff lightly, then sew to either side of the body at shoulder level. Partly sew the seams on the legs and feet, stuff quite firmly, then sew to either side of the body at the base. Use pink DK (8-ply) yarn to make a pompom tail, then attach to the rabbit's bottom.

Legs

Make two alike, worked in st st.
Using 4.0mm (UK 8, US 6) needles and shade A cast on 10 sts.
Purl 1 row.
Next row: inc in each st to end (20 sts).
Next row: purl.
Next row: inc in each st to end (40 sts).
Beginning with a purl row, work 11 rows in st st.

Shape the foot

Next row: k10, (k2tog) 10 times, k10 (30 sts).
Next row: purl.
Next row: k10, (k2tog) 5 times, k10 (25 sts).
Beginning with a purl row, work in st st for 19 rows
Next row: (k2tog) to last st, k1 (13 sts).
Next row: purl.
Next row: (k2tog) to last st, k1.
Break yarn and run through sts on needle, draw up and fasten off.

Pink overskirt

Using 4.0mm (UK 8, US 6) needles and yarn B cast on 40 sts.

Knit 2 rows.

Work 6 rows in st st.

Next row: inc in every st to end (80 sts).

Next row: purl.

Work 2 rows in st st.

Now work points entirely in garter stitch.

Next row: k10, turn and work the first point as follows.

Next row: k2tog at each end of next and following alt rows until you have 2 sts left.

K2tog and fasten off.

Return to remaining stitches and work across the next set of 10 sts in the same manner.

Continue to work on each subsequent group of 10 sts until you have worked 8 petal points in all.

Work in ends and sew back seam of skirt.

Green underskirt

Using 4.0mm (UK 8, US 6) needles and yarn C cast on 40 sts.

Knit 4 rows.

Work 4 rows in st st.

Next row: inc in every st to end (80 sts).

Next row: purl.

Work 2 rows in st st.

Now work points entirely in garter stitch.

Next row: k10, turn and work the first point as follows.

Next row: k2tog at each end of next and following alt rows until you have 2 sts left.

K2tog and fasten off.

Return to remaining stitches and work across the next set of 10 sts in the same manner.

Continue to work on each subsequent group of 10 sts until you have worked 8 petal points in all.

Work in all ends and sew back seam of underskirt.

Bodice

Using 4.0mm (UK 8, US 6) needles and yarn B cast on 26 sts.

Work 2 rows garter stitch.

Work 14 rows in st st.

Cast off 2 sts at beg of next 2 rows (22 sts).

Next row: k4, cast off 14, k to end.

Turn and work in garter stitch on the first set of 4 sts.

Work 30 rows, do not cast off but leave on a safety pin for now.

Return to the other set of 4 sts and work 29 rows.

Next row: k4 sts, turn and cast on 14 sts, turn and knit across 4 sts left on pin.

Turn and purl across all sts.

Cast on 2 sts at the beg of the next 2 rows.

Work 14 rows in st st.

Work 2 rows in garter stitch. Cast off.

Frills

Worked along the outside edge of each bodice strap.

Using 4.0mm (UK 8, US 6) needles and yarn B, with right side of piece facing, pick up and knit 30 sts along outside of one strap.

Knit 1 row.

Next row: inc in every st to end (60 sts).

Beginning with a purl row, work 3 rows in st st.

Break B and join in C.

Using C cast off firmly. Work the other frill in the same way on the other outside edge of the strap.

Work in all ends. Sew side seams and join frills at underarms. Take a needle threaded with green yarn and run a gathering thread all along the cast off edge of the sleeve, draw up to add gathers to the sleeve. Fasten off. Work the same on the other sleeve edge.

Necklace

Using 4.0mm (UK 8, US 6) needles and yarn C cast on 36 sts, knit 2 rows and cast off.

Rose for head

Using 4.0mm (UK 8, US 6) needles and yarn B cast on 26 sts.

Knit 1 row.

Next row: cast off next 2 sts as normal, * yrn, slip stitch on needle over yarn loop, knit next st and cast off in usual way, rep from * across row until all stitches are cast off. The piece of knitting will coil as you cast off.

Leaf

Worked in garter stitch.

Using 4.0mm (UK 8, US 6) needles and yarn C cast on 2 sts.

Next row: knit.

Next row: inc in next st, k1 (3 sts).

Next row: knit.

Next row: inc in first and last st (5 sts).

Knit 2 rows.

Next row: k2tog at each end of row (3 sts).

Next row: knit.

Next row: k3tog, fasten off.

Shoes

Make two alike, worked in garter stitch.

Using 4.0mm (UK 8, US 6) needles and yarn C cast on 23 sts.

Knit 1 row.

Next row: * k1, inc in next st, rep from * to last st, k1 (34 sts).

Next row: knit.

Next row: k16, m1, k2, m1, k16 (36 sts).

Next row: knit

Next row: k16, m1, k4, m1, k16 (38 sts).

Next row: knit.

Next row: k16, m1, k6, m1, k16 (40 sts).

Next row: knit.

Work 4 rows in garter stitch.

Next row: k9, (k2tog) five times, k2, (k2tog) five times, k9 (30 sts).

Next row: k10, cast off 10 sts, k to end.

Work on first set of 10 sts.

Next row: knit.

Next row: k2, yfwd, k2tog, k6.

Work 3 rows in garter stitch and cast off.

Rejoin yarn to remaining sts and complete to match first side, reversing position of hole.

Making up the accessories

Slip the top onto the rabbit. Catch the top of the frilled pieces to the shoulders of the rabbit on either side to hold them in place. Place the green skirt underneath the pink skirt and position so that the green points alternate with the pink points. Sew the skirt layers together. Slip the skirt onto the rabbit. Catch the base of the top to the waist of the skirt all the way around. Thread a length of ribbon through the fabric at the waist and tie into a neat bow.

Sew the back and foot seam of the shoes. Thread a length of ribbon through both holes at the top of the shoe, tie in a bow. Coil the rose into a neat shape and secure with a few stitches. Sew the leaf to the base of the rose. Sew the flower to the top of the rabbit's head. Sew a ribbon rose to the centre of the necklace. Place the band around the rabbit's neck and sew in place at the back of the neck.

Let's hop to the bunny beat!

Tiny Fluffy Bunny

This tiny little bunny will sit in the palm of your hand. He will take just a couple of hours to make so why not knit a whole family using this pattern? This is a simple knit, ideal for novice knitters.

Materials

50g (1¾oz) white chunky, fluffy yarn: 1 ball will make more than one rabbit; eyelash yarns can be substituted

Small amount of black DK (8-ply) yarn for embroidery

Small amount safety stuffing

Small piece of narrow ribbon

Needles

5.0mm (UK 6, US 8)

Tension (gauge)

15 sts x 20 rows measures 10 x 10cm (4 x 4in) using 5.0mm (UK 6, US 8) needles over st st

Size

14cm (5½in) long, 10cm (4in) tall

Notes

Rabbit is worked entirely in garter stitch.

Body

Using 5.0mm (UK 6, US 8) needles cast on 6 sts.
Next row: knit.
Next row: inc in each st to end (12 sts).
Next row: knit.
Next row: * k1, inc in next st, rep from * to end (18 sts).
Next row: knit.
Work 8 rows garter stitch.
Next row: * k1, k2tog, rep from * to end (12 sts).
Next row: knit.
Next row: (k2tog) across row (6 sts).
Knit 1 row. Cast off.

Head

Using 5.0mm (UK 6, US 8) needles cast on 3 sts.
Knit 1 row.
Next row: inc in every st (6 sts).
Next row: knit.
Next row: * k1, inc in next st, rep from * to end (9 sts).
Knit 5 rows.
Next row: * k1, k2tog, rep from * to end (6 sts).
Next row: knit.
Next row: (k2tog) across row (3 sts).
Next row: k3tog, fasten off.

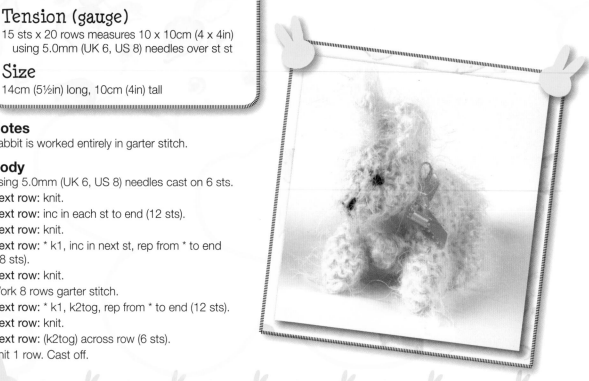

Ears

Make two alike.

Using 5.0mm (UK 6, US 8) needles cast on 3 sts.

Next row: knit.

Next row: inc 1 st at each end of next row (5 sts).

Knit 10 rows.

Next row: k2tog at each end of next row (3 sts).

Next row: k3tog, fasten off.

Feet

Make four alike.

Using 5.0mm (UK 6, US 8) needles cast on 5 sts.

Knit 10 rows.

K2tog at each end of next 2 rows (3 sts).

Next row: k3tog and fasten off.

Making up

Partly sew up the body seam, then stuff before closing. Sew up and stuff the head in the same way. Sew the head to the body. Partly sew the leg seams and stuff lightly before closing. Pin in place on the body of the rabbit then attach securely.

Sew the ears to either side of the head, pleating them at the base to give them shape. Embroider the face using black DK (8-ply) yarn. Wrap a small piece of narrow ribbon around the neck. Tie it into a neat bow and secure with a few stitches.

Make a small pompom using the white, fluffy yarn and attach to the rabbit's bottom.

Halloween Bunny

Take this pretty rabbit with you when you go trick-or-treating so that she can help you celebrate Halloween. Dress her in a black cape decorated with sparkly pumpkin and crescent moon buttons as a finishing touch.

Materials

100g (3½oz) orange DK (8-ply) yarn (A)
100g (3½oz) black DK (8-ply) yarn (B)
Black and white spotted ribbon
Pumpkin buttons
Safety stuffing

Needles

4.0mm (UK 8, US 6)

Tension (gauge)

22 sts x 30 rows measures 10 x 10cm (4 x 4in)
    using 4.0mm (UK 8, US 6) needles over st st

Size

18cm (7in) wide, 24cm (9½in) tall

Head

Worked in st st.
Using 4.0mm (UK 8, US 6) needles and yarn A cast on 10 sts.
Purl 1 row.
Next row: inc in each st to end (20 sts).
Beginning with a purl row, work 3 rows in st st.
Next row: * k1, inc, rep from * to end (30 sts).
Beginning with a purl row, work 5 rows in st st.
Next row: * k2, inc, rep from * to end (40 sts).
Beginning with a purl row, work 7 rows.
Next row: * k2, skpo, rep from * to end (30 sts).
Beginning with a purl row, work 3 rows in st st.

Next row: * k1, skpo, rep from * to end (20 sts).
Beginning with a purl row, work 3 rows in st st.
Next row: (k2tog) across row (10 sts).
Next row: purl.
Next row: (k2tog) five times, break yarn and run through sts on needle, draw up and fasten off.
This is the nose end of the piece.

Ears

Make two alike, worked entirely in garter stitch.
Using 4.0mm (UK 8, US 6) needles and yarn A cast on 5 sts.
Knit 2 rows.
Inc 1 st each end of next and following alt rows to 15 sts.
Work 47 rows in garter stitch.
Next row: k2tog at each end of row (13 sts).
Next row: knit.
Rep last 2 rows until you have 9 sts.
Work 1 row and cast off. This is the top of the ear.

Body

Worked in st st.
Using 4.0mm (UK 8, US 6) needles and yarn A cast on 10 sts.
Purl 1 row.
Next row: inc in each st to end (20 sts).
Beginning with a purl row, work 3 rows in st st.
Next row: * k1, inc, rep from * to end (30 sts).
Beginning with a purl row, work 3 rows in st st.
Next row: * k2, inc, rep from * to end (40 sts).
Beginning with a purl row, work 3 rows in st st.
Next row: * k3, inc, rep from * to end (50 sts).

Beginning with a purl row, work 11 rows.
Next row: * k3, skpo, rep from * to end (40 sts).
Beginning with a purl row, work 20 rows in st st.
Next row: purl.
Next row: * k2, skpo, rep from * to end (30 sts).
Next row: purl.
Next row: (k2tog) across row, break yarn and run through sts on needle, draw up and fasten off.

Legs

Make two alike, worked in st st.
Using needles size 4.0mm (UK 8, US 6) and yarn A cast on 10 sts.
Purl 1 row.
Next row: inc in each st to end (20 sts).
Next row: k1, inc in each of the next 18 sts, k1 (38 sts).
Beginning with a purl row, work 11 rows in st st.

Shape the foot

Next row: k9, (k2tog) 10 times, k9 (28 sts).
Next row: purl.
Next row: k9, (k2tog) five times, k9 (23 sts).
Beginning with a purl row, work 3 rows in st st.
Next row: k10, sl1, k2tog, psso, k10 (21 sts).
Beginning with a purl row, work 19 rows in st st.
Next row: (k2tog) across row, to last st, k1 (11 sts).
Next row: purl.
Next row: (k2tog) across row, break yarn and run through sts on needle, draw up and fasten off.

Arms

Make two alike, worked in st st.
Using 4.0mm (UK 8, US 6) needles and yarn A cast on 10 sts.
Purl 1 row.
Next row: k1, inc in each st to last st, k1 (18 sts).
Beginning with a purl row, work 3 rows in st st.
Next row: k1, * inc, k2, rep from * to last 2 sts, inc, k1 (24 sts).
Beginning with a purl row, work 29 rows in st st.
Next row: k1, * sl1, k1, psso, k2, rep from * to last st, k1 (18 sts).
Beginning with a purl row, work 3 rows of st st.
Next row: k1, * inc in next st, k1, rep from * to last st, k1 (26 sts).
Beginning with a purl row, work 7 rows of st st.
Next row: k2tog, * sl1, k1, psso, rep from * to last 2 sts, k2tog (13 sts).
Purl.
Next row: k1, (k2tog), across row. Cast off.

Cape

Using 4.0mm (UK 8, US 6) needles and yarn B cast on 30 sts.

Work 6 rows in garter stitch.

Next row: knit.

Next row: k5, purl to last 5 sts, k5.

Next row: k5, * k1, inc in next st, rep from * to last 5 sts, k5 (40 sts).

Next row: k5, purl to last 5 sts, k5.

Next row: knit.

Next row: k5, purl to last 5 sts, k5.

Next row: k5, * k2, inc in next st, rep from * to last 5 sts, k5 (50 sts).

Next row: k5, purl to last 5 sts, k5.

Next row: knit.

Next row: k5, purl to last 5 sts, k5.

Next row: k5, * k3, inc in next st, rep from * to last 5 sts, k5 (60 sts).

Continue to inc 10 sts on every 4th row as set, working 1 extra st before each inc, until there are 90 sts.

Next row: k5, purl to last 5 sts, k5.

Keeping 5 sts each end in garter stitch as before work 20 rows more.

Work 4 rows garter stitch

Join in A.

Knit 2 rows.

Knit 1 row in B and cast off.

Work in ends. Make a twisted cord using yarn A, thread through garter stitch at neck edge. Sew on sparkly pumpkin and crescent moon buttons to decorate the cape if desired.

Making up

Begin with the head. Work in the spare ends and partly sew the seam, stuffing firmly before closing. The seam will run underneath the head. Pleat the ears at the base and stitch to either side of the head. Embroider the nose, mouth and eyes using black DK (8-ply) yarn.

Partly sew the body seam, which runs down the centre of the rabbit's back. Stuff firmly then sew closed. Partly sew the seams on the arms and legs, stuffing each piece before closing. Add extra to the feet to give them a nice shape. Sew the arms and legs to the body. Remember to position the legs in a sitting position. Sew the head firmly to the body. Make a large pompom tail from yarn B and attach it to the back of the body.

Cut two lengths of ribbon. Tie each into a bow and then sew each bow to the top of one of the ears.

Bride and Groom

Make these delightful wedding rabbits as a special keepsake. You will need a little time and patience when putting the finishing touches to them, but the basic rabbits and clothes are simple to make. Please remember that because of the large amount of little pieces that are sewn on to the bride's dress, head and shoes these rabbits are not suitable as toys for little children.

Materials

100g (3½oz) brown DK (8-ply) yarn (A)
50g (1¾oz) dark grey DK (8-ply) yarn (B)
50g (1¾oz) light grey DK (8-ply) yarn (C)
50g (1¾oz) white DK (8-ply) yarn (D)
100g (3½oz) white, pearlescent DK (8-ply) yarn (E)
Small amount of black DK (8-ply) yarn
Small square of white net for veil
1m (3ft) fancy white satin ribbon
White and pink paper roses
7 white organza and pearl flowers
Tiny pink artificial flowers
Small amount of florists' tape
3 tiny heart pearl buttons
3 tiny brass buttons
16 small white ribbon roses
Narrow elastic
Safety stuffing

Needles

4.0mm (UK 8, US 6)

Tension (gauge)

22 sts x 30 rows measures 10 x 10cm (4 x 4in) using 4.0mm (UK 8, US 6) needles over st st

Size

20cm (8in) wide, 30cm (12in) tall

Head

For both bride and groom, worked in garter stitch.
Using 4.0mm (UK 8, US 6) needles and yarn A cast on 10 sts.
Knit 1 row.
Next row: inc in each st to end (20 sts).
Work 3 rows garter stitch.
Next row: * k1, inc, rep from * to end (30 sts).
Work 5 rows garter stitch.
Next row: * k2, inc, rep from * to end (40 sts).
Work 3 rows garter stitch.
Next row: * k3, inc, rep from * to end (50 sts).
Work 5 rows garter stitch.
Next row: * k3, skpo, rep from * to end (40 sts).
Work 3 rows garter stitch.
Next row: * k2, skpo, rep from * to end (30 sts).
Work 3 rows garter stitch.
Next row: * k1, skpo, rep from * to end (20 sts).
Work 3 rows garter stitch.
Next row: (k2tog) across row (10 sts).
Next row: knit.
Next row: (k2tog) five times, break yarn and run through sts on needle, draw up and fasten off. This is the nose end of the piece.

Arms

For both bride and groom, make two per rabbit, worked in garter stitch.

Using 4.0mm (UK 8, US 6) needles and yarn A cast on 8 sts.

Knit 1 row.

Next row: inc in every st (16 sts).

Knit 2 rows.

Inc 1 st at each end of next and alt rows until there are 22 sts.

Knit 20 rows.

Decrease for top of arm.

Next row: k2tog at each end of row (14 sts).

Next row: knit.

Next row: (k2tog) across row (7 sts).

Cast off. This is the top of the arm.

Groom's body

Make back and front alike, worked in garter stitch.

Using 4.0mm (UK8, US 6) needles and yarn A cast on 16 sts.

Knit 4 rows.

Inc 1 st each end of next and following alt rows until there are 26 sts.

Work 36 rows in garter stitch.

Dec 1 st each end of next and following alt rows until 14 sts remain. Cast off. This is the neck edge.

Groom's legs

Make two, worked in garter stitch.

Using 4.0mm (UK 8, US 6) needles and yarn A cast on 16 sts.

Knit 1 row.

Inc in every st to end (32 sts).

Work 12 rows garter stitch.

Next row: k11, (k2tog) 5 times, k11 (27 sts).

Knit 26 rows.

Next row: k2tog at each end of row (25 sts).

Next row: knit.

Next row: k1, (k2tog) across row (13 sts).

Cast off.

Bride and groom's ears

Make two for each rabbit, worked in garter stitch.

Using 4.0mm (UK 8, US 6) needles and yarn A cast on 8 sts.

Knit 2 rows.

Next row: inc 1 st at each of next and following alt row (12 sts).

Work 18 rows in garter stitch.

Next row: k2tog at each end of row (10 sts).

Next row: knit.

Repeat last 2 rows until 2 sts remain.

K2tog and fasten off.

Bride's body

Make back and front alike, worked in garter stitch.

Using 4.0mm (UK 8, US 6) needles and shade D cast on 16 sts.

Knit 4 rows.

Inc 1 st each end of next and following alt rows until there are 26 sts.

Work 18 rows in garter stitch.

Change to shade E and bodice pattern as follows:

Row 1: * k2, p2, rep from * to last 2 sts, k2.

Row 2: p2, * k2, p2, rep from * to end.

Row 3: as row 1.

Row 4: as row 1.

Row 5: as row 2.

Row 6: as row 1.

Bride's skirt

Make two pieces alike.

Using 4.0mm (UK 8, US 6) needles and yarn E cast on 56 sts.

Commence lacy pattern as follows:

Row 1: knit.

Row 2: purl.

Row 3: k1, * (k2tog) 3 times, (yrn, k1) 6 times, (k2tog) 3 times, rep from * to last st, k1.

Row 4: knit.

These 4 rows form the pattern and are repeated throughout.

Repeat them 11 more times.

Next row: (k2tog) across row (28 sts).

Work 4 rows garter stitch.

Cast off.

Work another piece to match.

Bride's sleeves

Make two alike.

Using 4.0mm (UK 8, US 6) needles and yarn E cast on 38 sts.

Commence lacy pattern as follows:

Row 1: knit.

Row 2: purl.

Row 3: k1, * (k2tog) 3 times, (yrn, k1) 6 times, (k2tog) 3 times, rep from * to last st, k1.

Row 4: knit.

These 4 rows form the pattern and are repeated throughout.

Repeat these 4 rows 3 times more.

Cast off.

Repeat these 6 rows twice more.

Keeping pattern correct dec 1 st each end of next and following alt rows until 14 sts remain. Cast off. This is the neck edge.

Bride's legs

Worked in garter stitch.

Using 4.0mm (UK 8, US 6) needles and D cast on 16 sts.

Knit 1 row.

Inc in every st to end (32 sts).

Work 12 rows garter stitch.

Next row: k11, (k2tog) five times, k11 (27 sts).

Knit 4 rows, break D and join in A.

Work a further 22 rows in garter stitch.

Next row: k2tog at each end of row (25 sts).

Next row: knit.

Next row: k1, (k2tog) across row (13 sts).

Cast off.

Waistcoat: back

Using needles size 4.0mm (UK 8, US 6) and yarn C cast on 36 sts, work 4 rows in garter stitch. Change to st st and work 18 rows.

Shape armholes

Cast off 4 sts at the beg of the next 2 rows.
Next row: knit.
Next row: k2, purl to last 2 sts, k2.
Continue as set by last 2 rows a further 9 times.
Work 4 rows garter stitch. Cast off.

Waistcoat: left front

Using 4.0mm (UK 8, US 6) needles and yarn C cast on 19 sts.
Work 4 rows garter stitch.
Next row: knit.
Next row: k3, purl to end.
Repeat the last 2 rows a further 9 times.
Cast off 4 sts, knit to end.
Next row: k3, purl to last 2 sts, k2.
Next row: k to last 5 sts, k2tog, k3.
Continue as set by last 2 rows until 6 sts remain.
Work 4 rows garter stitch, cast off.

Waistcoat: right front

Using 4.0mm (UK 8, US 6) needles and yarn C cast on 19 sts.
Work 4 rows garter stitch.
Next row: knit.
Next row: purl to last 3 sts, k3.
Repeat the last 2 rows for a further 8 times.
Then repeat row 1 again.
Cast off 4 sts, purl to last 3 sts, k3.
Next row: k3, k2tog tbl, knit to end.
Next row: k2, purl to last 3 sts, k3.
Continue as set by last 2 rows until 6 sts remain.
Work 4 rows garter stitch, cast off.

Sleeves

Make two alike.

Using 4.0mm (UK 8, US 6) needles and yarn D cast on 38 sts.

Work 6 rows in garter stitch.

Next row: cast off 3 sts, knit to end.

Continue in st st for 20 rows, cast off.

Trousers

Make two pieces alike.

Using 4.0mm (UK 8, US 6) needles and yarn B cast on 34 sts.

Work 4 rows garter stitch.

Change to st st and work 6 rows.

Next row: inc 1 st each end of next row (36 sts).

Next row: purl.

Work 2 rows in st st.

Cast on 3 sts at the beg of the next 2 rows (42 sts).

Work 3 rows in st st.

Cast on 2 sts at beg of next 2 rows (46 sts).

Work 3 rows in st st.

Next row: inc 1 st at each end (48 sts).

Next row: purl. Mark this row as end of leg shaping.

Work 10 rows in st st.

Change to k2, p2 rib and work 4 rows, cast off.

Cravat

Worked in moss stitch.

Using 4.0mm (UK 8, US 6) needles and yarn E cast on 15 sts.

Work in moss stitch for 10 rows.

Dec 1 st each end of next and following alt rows, until 7 sts remain.

Continue on these sts for a further 10cm (4in).

Inc 1 st each end of next and following alt rows until there are 15 sts.

Work 10 rows. Cast off.

Making up the rabbits

For each rabbit, partly sew the seam on the head, which runs underneath the piece. Stuff quite firmly, then sew closed. Using black DK (8-ply) yarn, embroider the eyes, nose and mouth. Pull the eyes in firmly to give shape to the face as you embroider them. Attach one ear to either side of the head, curling them slightly when stitching them, to give a pleasing shape.

Sew the body pieces together, leaving the neck edge open for stuffing. Stuff the body firmly and shape, then close the opening.

Sew up the arms – the seams will be at the centre back – leaving the top open to stuff. Shape as you stuff, then close. Sew up the legs – the seam is at the centre back, as on the arms. Leave the top of the leg open, stuff and shape, then sew up opening. Attach the arms and legs securely to the body. Make sure the legs are level on either side before stitching them. Make a pompom tail for each rabbit using white DK (8-ply) yarn and attach.

the ribbon into a rosette. Sew two organza and pearl flowers onto the top of the rosette. Cut a small circle of net and gather it into another rosette shape; secure with a few small stitches. Place the ribbon and flowers onto the net rosette and sew together. Sew the head dress onto the centre of the gathered top of the veil. Secure to the bride's head with a few stitches.

Making up the bouquet

Take some pink paper roses, tiny artificial flowers and three organza and pearl flowers and arrange them into a pleasing bouquet shape. Twist the wire stems together tightly. Use a little bit of floristry tape to bind the wires together and cover any sharp ends.

Sew the bride's hands together at the ends, then slot the bouquet into her hands.

Thread an organza and pearl flower through the front of each 'shoe' on the bride's legs.

Making up the dress

Sew the side seams, making sure that you align the pattern. Slip onto the bride rabbit. Take the ribbon and using a wide-eyed blunt-ended needle, thread the ribbon all around the waist, starting and ending at the centre back. Draw it through to fit around the waist, tie it in a bow, then trim the ends. Sew a ribbon rose to the centre of the bow and on each end of the ties. Secure the skirt in a few places around the waist.

Sew the sleeve seams then slip onto the rabbit's arms. Sew in place, catching the sleeves to the body. Sew a ribbon rose to the centre top of each sleeve. Sew three tiny heart buttons to the front of the bodice.

Making up the veil

Cut a piece of net into an oblong shape approximately 25 x 18cm (10 x 7in). Using a needle and fine thread, sew a small running stitch along one long edge, then gather the net and secure with a stitch. Set to one side. Take a short piece of ribbon approximately 13cm (5in) long and, using a small running stitch, sew along the centre of the length of the ribbon. Gather

Making up the trousers

Fold the leg pieces in half lengthways – the centre fold will be at the side of the leg. Sew the shaped section of the legs together, then the front and back seams. The trousers will look quite wide at this stage. Run narrow elastic through the rib section at the waist to draw them in to fit the rabbit. Slip onto the rabbit.

Making up the waistcoat

Sew the shoulder and side seams. Sew the sleeve seams, overlapping the cast-off garter stitch at the beginning of the sleeve and secure with a tiny pearl button. Sew the sleeves into waistcoat armholes, easing to fit if needed. Slip on to the groom rabbit. Sew three brass buttons onto the front band, catching the bands together as you sew. Sew the base of the waistcoat over the top of the trousers to keep it in place.

Making up the cravat

Work in the ends on the cravat. Place it around the groom's neck, overlapping the wide ends at the front and tucking them inside the top of the waistcoat. Pouch out a little. To complete the look, twist together three paper roses and wind a little bit of floristry tape around the base. Push through the waistcoat front and secure in place with a few stitches.

That's hoppily ever after!

Millie Bunny

Knit this sweet little bunny in just a couple of evenings; she is simple to make and measures just 20cm (8in) from her toes to the top of her head. She has a pretty striped top and a little skirt complete with straps, and to complete the set she also has a tiny pair of shoes.

Materials

50g (1¾oz) beige 4-ply (fingering) yarn (A)
Small amounts of white, pale blue and lemon
    yellow 4-ply (fingering) yarn
Small amount of black DK (8-ply) yarn
Safety stuffing
Four tiny blue buttons
Small amount of narrow blue ribbon

Needles

3.25mm (UK 10, US 3)

Tension (gauge)

27 sts x 36 rows measures 10 x 10cm (4 x 4in)
    using 3.25mm (UK 10, US 3) needles over st st

Size

12cm (5in) wide, 20cm (8in) tall

Head

Worked in st st.
Using 3.25mm (UK 10, US 3) needles and yarn A cast on 9 sts.
Purl 1 row.
Next row: inc knitwise in each st to end (18 sts).
Next row: purl.
Next row: * k1, inc in next st, rep from * to end (27 sts).
Next row: purl.
Work 8 rows in st st.
Next row: * k1, k2tog, rep from * to end (18 sts).

Next row: purl.
Next row: * k1, k2tog, rep from * to end (12 sts).
Next row: purl.
Next row: (k2tog) across row (6 sts).
Break yarn and thread through sts on needle, draw up and fasten off.

Body

Worked in st st.
Using 3.25mm (UK 10, US 3) needles and yarn A cast on 10 sts.
Next row: purl.
Next row: inc in each st to end (20 sts).
Beginning with a purl row, work 3 rows in st st.
Next row: * k1, inc in next st, rep from * to end (30 sts).
Work 17 rows in st st.
Next row: * k2, skpo, rep from * to last 2 sts, k2 (23 sts).
Next row: purl.
Next row: k1, * k2tog, rep from * to end (12 sts).
Next row: purl.
Next row: (k2tog) across row (6 sts).
Break yarn and run through sts on needle. Draw up and fasten off.

Ears

Make two alike, worked in garter stitch.
Using 3.25mm (UK 10, US 3) needles and yarn A cast on 6 sts.
Knit 2 rows.
Inc 1 st at each end of next and follow alt rows to 10 sts.
Work 20 rows in garter stitch.
Cast off.

Legs

Make two alike, worked in st st.

Using 3.25mm (UK 10, US 3) needles and yarn A cast on 12 sts.

Work in st st for 22 rows.

Next row: * k1, inc in next st, rep from * to end (18 sts).

Beginning with a purl row, work 7 rows in st st.

Next row: * k1, k2tog, rep from * to end (12 sts).

Next row: purl.

Next row: (k2tog) across row (6 sts).

Next row: purl.

Break yarn and thread through sts, draw up and fasten off.

Arms

Make two alike, worked in st st.

Using 3.25mm (UK 10, US 3) needles and yarn A cast on 6 sts.

Next row: purl.

Next row: inc at each end of next and following row to 12 sts.

Next row: purl.

Work 10 rows in st st.

Next row: * k1, inc in next st, rep from * to end (18 sts).

Work 5 rows in st st.

Next row: * k1, k2tog, rep from * to end (12 sts).

Next row: purl.

Next row: (k2tog) across row (6 sts).

Next row: purl.

Break yarn and thread through sts, draw up and fasten off.

Making up

Partly sew the body seam, which runs down the centre of the back. Stuff the body quite firmly before closing the seam completely. Partly sew the head seam, which runs underneath the piece; stuff as you did the body, then sew closed.

Take the ears and pleat the cast-off edges together to give shape. Sew an ear to either side of the head. Tie a small bow to the top of each ear. Take some black DK (8-ply) yarn and embroider the facial features. Sew the head to the body.

Partly sew the seams on the arms and legs, then stuff fairly firmly before closing. Flatten the ends of the arms and sew three little lines at the end of each to depict paws. Sew the arms and legs to body.

Millie's T-shirt

Knit back and front alike.

Using 3.25mm (UK 10, US 3) needles cast on 24 sts in white.

Work 3 rows in garter stitch.

Change to st st.

Work 2 rows white, 2 rows yellow, 2 rows white, 2 rows yellow.

Cast on 6 sts at beg of next 2 rows, using white.

Work 8 rows in stripe sequence. Work 4 rows garter stitch in white. Cast off.

Shoes

Make two alike, worked in garter stitch.

Using 3.25mm (UK 10, US 3) needles and blue yarn cast on 10 sts.

Knit 2 rows.

Inc in each st to end (20 sts).

Next row: knit.

Next row: * k1, inc, rep from * to end (30 sts).

Knit 8 rows.

Decrease for top

Next row: k13, (k2tog), twice, k13 (28 sts).

Next row: k12, (k2tog), twice, k12 (26 sts).

Next row: knit.

Next row: k8, cast off 10 sts, k to end.

Next row: k8, cast on 8 sts, turn.

Next row: k16.

Cast off 16 sts.

Return to remaining 8 sts.

Knit to end.

Next row: knit.

Cast off.

Sew the seam on the foot. Turn one shoe inside out to reverse the strap on the shoe. Sew on a tiny button to secure the strap. Add a small amount of stuffing to the toe of the shoe, push the foot into the shoe and secure with a few stitches.

Sleeve edgings

Join shoulder seams.

Using 3.25mm (UK 10, US 3) needles and white yarn, with right sides facing, pick up and knit 24 sts along sleeve edge. Knit 1 row and cast off.

Repeat for other sleeve edging.

Sew side and sleeve seams. Slip onto rabbit.

Skirt

Using 3.25mm (UK 10, US 3) needles and blue yarn cast on 54 sts.

Work 6 rows in garter stitch.

Work 12 rows in st st.

Work 4 rows in k1, p1 rib.

Cast off in rib.

Straps

Make two.

Using 3.25mm (UK 10, US 3) needles and blue yarn, cast on 26 sts. Knit 1 row and cast off.

Sew seam on skirt: this runs down the centre back. Attach straps, crossing at the back. Sew tiny buttons to the straps on the front of the skirt. Embroider a tiny yellow flower onto one side of the front of the skirt.

Tweedy Bunny

With her cute dress complete with useful pockets and pretty motif, Alice will be the perfect friend for any little girl. The bunny is worked in just garter stitch and stocking stitch and is so easy to knit that even a novice can make her.

Materials
100g (3½oz) variegated brown and grey
   DK (8-ply) yarn (A)
100g (3½oz) variegated pink, blue, white and
   purple DK (8-ply) yarn (B)
Small amounts of black and white DK (8-ply) yarn
Rabbit motif (optional)
Safety stuffing

Needles
4.0mm (UK 8, US 6)

Tension (gauge)
22 sts x 28 rows measures 10 x 10cm (4 x 4in)
   using 4.0mm (UK 8, US 6) needles over st st

Size
16cm (6in) wide, 36cm (14½in) tall

Body and legs
Make back and front alike, worked in garter stitch.
Using 4.0mm (UK 8, US 6) needles and yarn A cast on 12 sts.
Next row: knit.
Next row: inc 1 st at each end (14 sts).
Next row: knit.
Next row: inc 1 st at each end (16 sts).
Next row: knit.
Continue in garter stitch for a further 44 rows.

Divide for legs
Next row: k8, turn. Work on these sts for first leg (leave remaining 8 sts on a holder).
Work 34 rows in garter stitch.
Next row: * k1, inc in next st, rep from * to end (12 sts).
Knit 2 rows.
Inc 1 st at each end of next and following alt row (16 sts).
Knit 10 rows.
Dec 1 st at each end of next and following alt rows to 6 sts.
Cast off.
Rejoin yarn to remaining 8 sts and work to match first leg.
Make another piece to match.

Head

Worked in garter stitch.
Using 4.0mm (UK 8, US 6) needles and yarn A cast on 8 sts.
Next row: knit.
Next row: inc in every st (16 sts).
Next row: knit.
Next row: * k1, inc in next st, rep from * to end (24 sts).
Knit 3 rows.
Next row: * k2, inc in next st, rep from * to end (32 sts).
Work 16 rows in garter stitch.
Next row: * k2, skpo, rep from * to end (24 sts).
Next row: knit.
Next row: * k1, skpo, rep from * to end (16 sts).
Next row: (k2tog) across row (8 sts).
Next row: knit, break yarn and run through sts on needle. Draw up and fasten off.

Ears

Make two alike, worked in garter stitch.
Using 4.0mm (UK 8 , US 6) needles and yarn A cast on 6 sts.
Next row: knit.
Inc 1 st at each end of the next and following alt rows to 10 sts.
Work 26 rows in garter stitch.
Next row: (k2tog) across row (5 sts).
Next row: (k2tog) twice, k1 (3 sts).
Next row: k3tog.
Fasten off.

Arms

Make two alike, worked in garter stitch.
Using 4.0mm (UK 8, US 6) needles and yarn A cast on 6 sts.
Knit 1 row.
Inc 1 st at each end of next and following alt rows to 12 sts.
Work 24 rows in garter stitch.
Next row: * k1 inc in next st, rep from * to end (18 sts).
Knit 5 rows.
Next row: * k1, k2tog, rep from * to end (12 sts).
Next row: knit.
Next row: * k1, k2tog, rep from * to end (8 sts).
Next row: knit.
Cast off.

Pockets

Make two alike, worked in garter stitch.

Using 4.0mm (UK 8, US 6) needles and yarn B, cast on 8 sts.

Work 14 rows in garter stitch.

Cast off.

Making up

Sew the back and front pieces of the body and legs together, leaving the neck edge open. Stuff evenly and fairly firmly before closing. Partly sew the arm seams and the head seam, which runs on the underside of the head, then stuff all the pieces fairly firmly before closing up all the seams. Pleat the cast-off edge of each ear to give shape, then sew in place on top of the head. Make a large pompom tail using white DK (8-ply) yarn and attach to the back of the body.

Embroider the facial features using black DK (8-ply) yarn. Sew the head to the body, then sew the arms to the body on either side at shoulder level. Sew the side seams of the dress, leaving an opening for the arm holes. Sew pockets onto either side at the lower front of the dress. Attach a motif to the front of the dress if required. Slip the dress onto the rabbit.

Dress

Make back and front alike.

Using 4.0mm (UK 8, US 6) needles and yarn B, cast on 30 sts.

Work 3 rows garter stitch.

Change to st st and continue until work measures 13cm (5in), ending on a purl row.

Next row: (k2tog) across row (15 sts).

Work 3 rows garter stitch.

Cast off.

Valentine's Bunny

This bunny has a message to bring along with her on Valentine's day! She is made in soft furry yarn and carries a red heart in her paws. Make her as a surprise to bring a big smile to the face of somebody special. She is quite easy to make, but the heart might require a little more time and patience.

Materials
100g (3½oz) cream fashion fur yarn (A)
50g (1¾oz) red DK (8-ply) yarn (B)
Small amount of green DK (8-ply) yarn (C)
Small amount of black DK (8-ply) yarn
Safety stuffing
A length of red satin ribbon

Needles
5.5mm (UK 5, US 9)
4.0mm (UK 8, US 6)
3.25mm (UK 10, US 3)

Tension (gauge)
12 sts x 16 rows measure 10 x 10cm (4 x 4in) using 5.5mm (UK 5, US 9) needles over st st

Size
22cm (8¾in) wide, 35cm (14in) tall

Notes
It isn't very easy to count rows on this type of yarn so I suggest you make a note of each row as you work it.

Head and body
Worked in st st.
Using 5.5mm (UK 5, US 9) needles and yarn A cast on 8 sts.
Work 2 rows in st st.
Next row: inc in each st (16 sts).
Next row: purl.
Next row: inc in each st (32 sts).

Work 3 rows in st st.
Next row: k1, * inc in next st, k1, rep from * to last st, k1 (47 sts).
Continue in st st for 25cm (10in).

Shape head
Next row: k1, * k1, k2tog, rep from * to last st, k1 (32 sts).
Beginning with a purl row, work 3 rows.
Next row: k1, * k1, k2tog, rep from * to last st, k1 (22 sts).
Next row: purl.
Next row: (k2tog) across row (11 sts).
Next row: purl.
Next row: (k2tog) across row to last st, k1 (6 sts).
Break yarn and run through stitches on needle. Draw up and fasten off.

Legs
Make two alike, worked in st st.
Using 5.5mm (UK 5, US 9) needles and yarn A cast on 8 sts.
Next row: purl.
Next row: inc knitwise in each st to end (16 sts).
Work 5 rows in st st.
Next row: inc 1 st at each end of row (18 sts).
Work 3 rows in st st.
Next row: * k2, inc in next st, rep from * to end (24 sts).
Work 13 rows in st st.
Next row: k9, inc in each of next 6 sts, k9 (30 sts).
Next row: purl.
Next row: k12, inc in each of next 6 sts, k12 (36 sts).

Beginning with a purl row, work 5 rows in st st.
Next row: (k2tog) across row (18 sts).
Next row: purl.
Next row: (k2tog) across row (9 sts).
Next row: purl.
Break yarn and run through stitches on needle, draw up and fasten off.

Arms

Make two alike, worked in st st.
Using 5.5mm (UK 5, US 9) needles and yarn A cast on 8 sts.
Next row: purl.
Next row: inc in each st (16 sts).
Next row: purl.
Work 4 rows in st st.
Next row: inc 1 st at each end of row (18 sts).
Beginning with a purl row, work 11 rows in st st.
Next row: * k2, inc in next st, rep from * to end (24 sts).
Beginning with a purl row, work 7 rows in st st.
Next row: (k2tog) across row (12 sts).
Next row: purl.
Next row: (k2tog) across row (6 sts).
Next row: purl.

Break yarn and run through sts on needle, draw up and fasten off.

Outer ears

Make two alike, worked in st st.
Using 5.5mm (UK 5, US 9) needles and yarn A cast on 8 sts.
Next row: purl.
Next row: inc 1 st at each end of row (10 sts).
Next row: purl.
Next row: inc 1 st at each end of row (12 sts).
Next row: purl.
Work in st st for 10cm (4in) ending with a purl row.

Decrease for top

Next row: k2tog at each end of row (10 sts).
Next row: purl.
Repeat last 2 rows until you have 2 sts.
K2tog and fasten off.

Inner ears

Make two alike, worked in st st.
Using 4.0mm (UK 8, US 6) needles and yarn B cast on 12 sts.
Work in st st for 28 rows.
Dec as for top of outer ears.

Muzzle

Worked in st st.
Using 5.5mm (UK 5, US 9) needles and yarn A cast on 6 sts.
Next row: purl.
Next row: inc in each st to end (12 sts).

Next row: purl.
Next row: inc 1 st at each end of row (14 sts).
Next row: purl.
Work 4 rows in st st.
Next row: dec 1 st at each end of next and following alt rows to 6 sts.
Cast off.

Nose

Worked in st st.
Using 4.0mm (UK 8, US 6) needles and yarn B, cast on 8 sts.
Work 6 rows in st st.
Dec 1 st at each end of next and following alt rows until you have 4 sts.
Next row: (k2tog) twice (2 sts).
Next row: k2tog, fasten off, leave a long tail of yarn.

Heart cushion

Make back and front alike, worked in st st with garter stitch edges. When beginning the heart you will make the increases using the 'inc' method, then change to the 'm1' method for the rest of the heart (see page 12).
Using 3.25mm (UK 10, US 3) needles and yarn B cast on 3 sts.
Knit 2 rows.
Next row: inc 1, k1, inc 1 (5 sts).
Next row: k2, p1, k2.
Next row: k1, inc, k1, inc, k1 (7 sts).

Next row: k2, p3, k2.
Next row: k2, m1, k3, m1, k2 (9 sts).
Next row: k2, p5, k2.
Next row: k2, m1, k5, m1, k2 (11 sts).
Next row: k2, p7, k2.
Continue increasing as before on every alternate row, until you have 33 sts on the needle.
Work 9 rows straight in st st keeping the 2 sts either end in garter stitch as before, ending on a purl row.

Divide for heart
Next row: k15, k2tog, turn (16 sts).
Next row: purl to last 2 sts, k2.
Next row: k2, k2tog, knit to last 2 sts, k2tog (14 sts).
Next row: purl to last 4 sts, p2tog, k2 (13 sts).
Next row: k2, k2tog, knit to last 2 sts, k2tog (11 sts).
Next row: purl to last 2 sts, k2.
Next row: k2, k2tog, knit to last 2 sts, k2tog (9 sts).
Next row: p2tog, purl to last 4 sts, p2tog, k2 (7 sts).
Cast off.
Rejoin yarn to remaining sts and work to match other side.

Rose
Using 4.0mm (UK 8, US 6) needles and yarn B cast on 35 sts.
Next row: k2, * cast off a st in the normal way, yrn, now lift the st on the needle over the yarn forward, k1, rep from * until all stitches are cast off.

Leaves
Using 4.0mm (UK 8, US 6) needles and yarn C cast on 45 sts.
Cast off.

Making up the rabbit

Sew the body and head seam leaving the base open to stuff. Stuff the head quite firmly and shape into a nice rounded ball. Measure 14cm (5½in) down from the top of the head and mark this row all around the neck. Take a needle threaded with yarn A and run through each stitch on the marked row, beginning and ending at the centre back seam. Draw up firmly to make the head. Secure the yarn to ensure the stitches don't pull out. Stuff the body and finally close the base.

Partly sew the seam on the arms – the seam runs on the underneath. Stuff fairly firmly. Sew to body on either side at shoulder height. Sew the legs in the same way – stuff as before, making sure that you put extra stuffing in the feet. Sew the legs to the body on either side in a sitting position. Make a large pompom tail from yarn B and attach it to the back of the body.

Take the muzzle and pin it to the front of the head, adding stuffing to pad it out. Sew it in place. Take the nose and sew it onto the centre of the muzzle. Use the tail of yarn and sew through the muzzle to create a mouth line – pull quite tight to create the cheeks of the rabbit on either side. Using black DK (8-ply) yarn, embroider the eyes. Sew the ears together in pairs, one red and one white. Pleat the base of each ear, then sew to the top of the rabbit's head.

Making up the heart

To make the heart, sew the two pieces together, leaving one side open, then stuff quite firmly before closing. Coil the rose into a neat flower shape and secure in the centre with a few stitches. Take the leaf piece and fold it in half, joining the ends, then sew the ends into loops to form leaves. Attach to the base of the rose. Sew the rose to the centre of the heart. Secure the heart in place by sewing the rabbit's paws to either side of it. Tie a red ribbon bow around the rabbit's neck to complete.

Bean Bag Bunny

Two-tone pink stripes and long floppy ears give this bunny a cute, modern look.
I have placed a small bag full of dried beans inside the base of the bunny's
body, so that it will sit upright – make sure that both the bean bag and bunny
are securely stitched up, so that the beans do not present a choking hazard for
children. If you would rather, you can simply fill the bunny with stuffing.

Materials
50g (1¾oz) light pink DK (8-ply) yarn (A)
50g (1¾oz) dark pink DK (8-ply) yarn (B)
Small amount of black DK (8-ply) yarn
Safety stuffing
Dried beans or peas for bean bag
Piece of calico fabric
Safety stuffing

Needles
4.0mm (UK 8, US 6)

Tension (gauge)
22 sts x 28 rows measures 10 x 10cm (4 x 4in)
    using 4.0mm (UK 8, US 6) needles over st st

Size
14cm (5½in) wide, 20cm (8in) tall

Notes
Rabbit is worked in st st in a stripe sequence of
4 rows A and 4 rows B throughout.

Body – begin at neck edge
Using 4.0mm (UK 8, US 6) needles and yarn A cast
on 10 sts.
Work 2 rows in st st.
Next row: inc in each st to end (20 sts).
Next row: purl.
Change to yarn B.

Next row: * k1, inc in next st, rep from * to end
(30 sts).
Beginning with a purl row, work 3 rows in st st.
Change to yarn A.
Next row: * k2, inc in next st, rep from * to end
(40 sts).
Beginning with a purl row, work 3 rows in st st.
Change to yarn B.
Work 2 rows in st st.
Next row: * k3, inc in next st, rep from * to end
(50 sts).
Next row: purl.
Change to yarn A.
Work 4 rows in st st.
Change to yarn B.
Work 4 rows in st st.
Change to yarn A.

Work 4 rows in st st.
Change to yarn B.
Work 4 rows in st st.
Change to yarn A.
Work 4 rows in st st.
Change to yarn B.
Work 2 rows in st st.
Next row: * k3, k2tog, rep from * to end (40 sts).
Next row: purl.
Change to yarn A.
Next row: * k2, k2tog, rep from * to end (30 sts).
Next row: purl.
Next row: * k1, k2tog, rep from * to end (20 sts).
Next row: purl.
Break yarn, thread through sts on needle, draw up and fasten off.

Head
Using 4.0mm (UK 8, US 6) needles and yarn B cast on 8 sts.
Next row: purl.
Next row: inc knitwise in each st to end (16 sts).
Next row: purl.
Change to yarn A.
Work 2 rows in st st.
Next row: * k2, inc in next st, rep from * to last st, k1 (21 sts).
Next row: purl.
Change to yarn B.
Work 2 rows in st st.
Next row: * k2, inc in next st, rep from * to end (28 sts).
Next row: purl.
Change to yarn A.
Work 4 rows in st st.

Change to yarn B.
Next row: * k3, inc in next st, rep from * to end (35 sts).
Next row: purl.
Work 2 rows in st st.
Change to yarn A.

Decrease for top
Next row: * k3, k2tog, rep from * to end (28 sts).
Next row: purl.
Next row: * k2, k2tog, rep from * to end (21 sts).
Next row: purl.
Change to yarn B.
Next row: * k1, k2tog, rep from * to end (14 sts).
Next row: purl.
Next row: (k2tog) across row (7 sts).
Next row: purl.

Change to yarn A.

Next row: (k2tog) across row to last st, k1 (4 sts).

Next row: purl, break yarn, run through sts on needle and fasten off.

Ears

Make two alike.

Using 4.0mm (UK 8, US 6) needles and yarn B cast on 6 sts.

Next row: purl.

Next row: * inc in next st, rep from * to end (12 sts).

Next row: purl.

Change to yarn A.

Work 4 rows in st st.

Change to yarn B.

Next row: * k1, inc in next st, rep from * to end (18 sts).

Beginning with a purl row, work 3 rows in st st.

Change to yarn A.

Next row: * k1, inc in next st, rep from * to end (27 sts).

Beginning with a purl row, work 3 rows in st st.

Continue in st st and work 4 rows B, 4 rows A and 4 rows B.

Change to yarn A.

Next row: * k2, skpo, rep from * to last 3 sts, k3 (21 sts).

Beginning with a purl row, work 3 rows in st st.

Change to yarn B.

Next row: * k1, skpo, rep from * to end (14 sts).

Next row: purl.

Next row: * k1, skpo, rep from * to last 2 sts, k2 (10 sts).

Next row: purl.

Change to yarn A.

Next row: * k1, skpo, rep from * to last st, k1 (7 sts).

Next row: purl.

Next row: (k2tog) 3 times, k1 (4 sts).

Next row: p4tog and fasten off.

Arms

Make two alike.

Using 4.0mm (UK 8, US 6) needles and yarn A cast on 8 sts.

Next row: purl.

Next row: inc in each st to end (16 sts).

Work 2 rows in st st.

Beginning with yarn B, work in st st, 4 rows B, 4 rows A, for a further 24 rows.

Change to yarn B.

Next row: * k2, inc in next st, rep from * to last st, k1 (21 sts).

Next row: purl.

Work 2 rows in st st.

Change to yarn A.

Work 4 rows in st st.

Change to yarn B.

Next row: * k1, k2tog, rep from * to end (14 sts).

Next row: purl.

Next row: (k2tog) across row. Break yarn and thread through sts on needle. Draw up and fasten off.

Legs

Make two alike, beginning at base of foot.

Using 4.0mm (UK 8, US 6) needles and yarn B cast on 15 sts.

Next row: purl.

Next row: * inc in each st to end (30 sts).

Next row: purl.

Change to yarn A.

Work 2 rows in st st.

Next row: * k3, inc in next st, rep from * to last 2 sts, k1, inc in last st (38 sts).

Next row: purl.

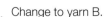

Change to yarn B.

Work 4 rows in st st.

Change to yarn A.

Work 4 rows in st st.

Shape foot

Change to yarn B.

Next row: k12, (skpo) 7 times, k12 (31 sts).

Next row: purl.

Next row: k11, (skpo) twice, k1, (skpo) twice, k11 (27 sts).

Next row: purl.

Change to yarn A.

Next row: k7, (skpo) 3 times, k1, (skpo) 3 times, k7 (21 sts).

Next row: purl.

Work 2 rows in st st.

Change to yarn B.

Work 4 rows in st st.

Change to yarn A.
+ Work 4 rows in st st.
Change to yarn B.
+ Work 4 rows in st st.
Change to yarn A.
+ Work 4 rows in st st.
Change to yarn B.
+ Work 4 rows in st st.
Change to yarn A.

Shape top

Next row: (k2tog) 10 times, k1 (11 sts).
Next row: purl.
Next row: (k2tog) 5 times, k1.
Break yarn and run through sts on needle, draw up
and fasten off.

Making up

If you intend to make the bean bag version of the
bunny, first make the calico bag that will contain the
beans. Cut a piece of calico 18 x 9cm (7 x 3½in), fold

in half lengthwise and seam the two long sides. Fill
with dried beans or peas, then sew the top section of
the piece very securely to ensure no beans will fall out.

Sew the body seam, which will run down the back
of the rabbit; before closing completely, insert the
bean bag and pack a little stuffing around it. Sew the
seam on the head, which runs on the underside. Stuff
firmly before closing. Using black DK (8-ply) yarn,
embroider the features.

Fold each ear in half, then sew the seam. Flatten
out so the seam will run down the centre back of the
piece. Sew both ears to the top of the head.

Sew the seams on the arms, stuffing before
closing completely, pushing extra into the hand
sections. Sew an arm to each side of the body at
shoulder height. Sew the seam on the legs and feet
in the same way, stuffing the feet quite firmly. Sit the
bunny on the edge of a flat surface, such as a table or
shelf, then pin the legs in place so they dangle. Sew
securely in position. Make a pompom tail from yarn A
and attach to the back of the body.

I'm crazy for carrots!

Party Bunny

With her pretty dress and cute bow this bunny is all ready for an outing! She is just waiting for a new friend and is sure to bring a smile to any child's face. Knitted in a soft yarn she is super cuddly. Simple stitches are used to make both the rabbit and her dress, so even novice knitters can try their hand at making her.

Materials
100g (3½oz) cream DK (8-ply) yarn (A)
50g (1¾oz) lime green DK (8-ply) yarn (B)
50g (1¾oz) denim blue DK (8-ply) yarn (C)
Small amount of white DK (8-ply) yarn for pompom tail
Small amount of black DK (8-ply) yarn
Safety stuffing
Matching ribbon and buttons

Needles
4.0mm (UK 8, US 6)

Tension (gauge)
22 sts x 28 rows measures 10 x 10cm (4 x 4in) using 4.0mm (UK 8, US 6) needles over st st

Size
25cm (10in) wide, 48cm (19¼in) tall

Head
Worked in st st.
Begin at back of head.
Using 4.0mm (UK 8, US 6) needles and yarn A cast on 10 sts.
Next row: purl.
Next row: k1, (m1, k1) to end (19 sts).
Next row: purl.

Repeat last 2 rows once more (37 sts).
Beginning with a knit row, work 7 rows in st st.
Next row: k2, (m1, k3) to last 2 sts, m1, k2 (49 sts).
Beginning with a purl row, work for 19 rows in st st.
Next row: k1, (k2tog) to end (25 sts).
Beginning with a purl row, work 7 rows in st st.
Next row: k1, (k2tog) across row (13 sts).
Next row: purl.
Break yarn and run through remaining stitches on needle, gather up and secure (this is the nose end of the rabbit).

Body
Worked in st st.
Using 4.0mm (UK 8, US 6) needles and yarn A cast on 13 sts (this is the neck edge).
Work 2 rows in st st.
Next row: k1, (m1, k1) across row (25 sts).
Beginning with a purl row, work 5 rows in st st.
Next row: k1, (m1, k1) to end (49 sts).
Beginning with a purl row, work 27 rows in st st.
Next row: k1, k2tog, rep from * to last st, k1 (33 sts).
Beginning with a purl row, work 5 rows in st st.
Next row: k1, (k2tog) across row (17 sts).
Beginning with a purl row, work 3 rows in st st.
Next row: k1, (k2tog) across row (9 sts).
Break yarn and thread through sts on needle. Draw up and fasten off.

Arms

Make two alike, worked in st st.

Using 4.0mm (UK 8, US 6) needles and yarn A cast on 10 sts.

Purl 1 row.

Next row: k1, inc in each st to last st, k1 (18 sts).

Beginning with a purl row, work 3 rows in st st.

Next row: k1, * inc in next st, k2, rep from * to last 2 sts, inc, k1 (24 sts).

Beginning with a purl row, work in st st for 21 rows.

Next row: k1, * skpo, k2, rep from * to last 3 sts, k3 (19 sts).

Beginning with a purl row, work 3 rows in st st.

Next row: k1, * inc in next st, k1, rep from * to last 2 sts, k2 (27 sts).

Beginning with a purl row, work 7 rows in st st.

Next row: k1, (skpo) across row to last 2 sts (15 sts).

Purl 1 row.

Next row: k1, (k2tog) across row. Cast off.

Legs and feet

Make two alike, worked in st st, beginning at base of foot.

Using 4.0mm (UK 8, US 6) needles and yarn A cast on 20 sts.

Purl 1 row.

Next row: k1, inc in each of the next 18 sts, k1 (38 sts).

Beginning with a purl row, work 11 rows in st st.

Shape the foot

Next row: k9, (k2tog) 10 times, k9 (28 sts).

Next row: purl.

Next row: k9, (k2tog) 5 times, K9 (23 sts).

Beginning with a purl row, work in st st for 27 rows.

Next row: * k1, k2tog, rep from * to last 2 sts, k2 (16 sts).

Next row: purl.

Next row: (k2tog) across row (8 sts).

Next row: purl.

Break yarn and run through sts on needle, draw up and fasten off.

Ears

Make two alike, worked in st st.

Using 4.0mm (UK 8, US 6) needles and yarn A cast on 24 sts.

Work 20 rows in st st.

Next row: k6, skpo, k8, k2tog, k6 (22 sts).

Next row: purl.

Next row: k2tog, k4, skpo, k6, k2tog, k4, skpo (18 sts).

Next row: purl.

Next row: k2tog, k3, skpo, k4, k2tog, k3, skpo (14 sts).

Next row: purl.

Next row: k2tog, k2, skpo, k2, k2tog, k2, skpo (10 sts).

Next row: purl.

Next row: k2tog, k1, skpo, k2tog, k1, k2tog (6 sts).

Next row: purl.

Cast off.

Making up

Work in all the ends neatly. Take the head and sew the seam from the nose to the back of the head, stuffing as you go. Shape the head and stuff quite firmly. Finally, close and secure. Seam the body piece together, remembering that the seam goes down the centre of the rabbit's back. Stuff from both ends to give a nice rounded shape. Close the ends neatly.

Sew the seams of the feet and legs – the seams run down the centre back. Stuff to give a nice shape; flatten the tops of the legs to enable you to stitch them to the body. Sew the arm seams and stuff, shaping as you do. Finally, close them.

Sew the ears – the seam is at centre back. Fold the ends of the ears together to give shape, then stitch to either side of head. Using the photographs as a guide, create the face. The eyes are worked with black DK (8-ply) yarn. Pull the yarn back and forth quite firmly through both eyes to shape the head. The nose is a 'Y' shape, connected to small lines for the mouth. Stitch the legs and arms to the body and finally position the head and sew firmly in place.
Make a white pompom tail and secure in place.

Dress: front

Using 4.0mm (UK 8, US 6) needles and yarn B cast on 72 sts.

Work 6 rows in garter stitch. Join yarn C.

Continue in stripe pattern:

Rows 1–4: using C work 4 rows in st st.

Rows 5–6: using B work 2 rows in garter stitch.

Repeat the last 6 rows until work measures approx. 10cm (4in) ending on a row 4.

Break C.

Continue in B only.

Next row: (k2tog) across row (36 sts).

Next row: knit.

Next row: (make holes for ribbon) k1, * yfwd, k2tog, rep from * to last st, k1.

Next row: knit.

Work 6 rows in st st.

Shape armholes

Cast off 3 sts at beg of next 2 rows (30 sts).

Next row: k1, skpo, knit to last 3 sts, k2tog, k1 (28 sts).

Next row: k1, purl to last st, k1. ***

Repeat last 2 rows until 20 sts remain, ending with a purl row.

Shape neck

Next row: k1, skpo, k4, turn (leave remaining sts on a stitch holder or spare needle) (6 sts).

Next row: p2tog, purl to last st, k1 (5 sts).

Next row: k1, skpo, k2 (4 sts).

Next row: p2tog, purl to end (3 sts).

Next row: skpo, k1 (2 sts).

Next row: p2tog. Fasten off.

Return to stitches on holder.

Slip centre 6 sts onto holder for centre neck, rejoin yarn to remaining sts and complete to match other side, working k2tog instead of skpo.

Dress: back

Work as front to ***

Next row: k1, skpo, k12, turn (proceed on this set of sts, leave remaining stitches on a holder) (14 sts).

Next row: k2, purl to last st, k1.

Next row: k1, skpo, knit to end (13 sts).

Next row: k2, purl to last st, k1.

Continue as set by last 2 rows until you have 6 sts left. Leave on a stitch holder.

Rejoin yarn to remaining sts and complete to match first side reversing shapings and working k2tog instead of skpo.

Sleeves

Make two alike.

Using 4.0mm (UK 8, US 6) needles and yarn B cast on 32 sts.

Work 3 rows in garter stitch.

Change to st st and work 8 rows.

Shape armholes

Cast off 3 sts at beg of next 2 rows (26 sts).

Next row: knit to end.

Next row: k1, purl to last st, k1.

Repeat last 2 rows once more.

Next row: k1, skpo, knit to last 3 sts.

K2tog, k1 (24 sts).

Next row: k1, purl to last st, k1.

Continue as set by last 2 rows until you have 10 sts left.

Cast off.

Neckband

Sew raglan seams on back, front and sleeves.

With right side of work facing, using 4.0mm (UK 8, US 6) needles and yarn C beginning at left back, pick up and knit 6 sts from left back, 10 sts from first sleeve, 5 sts down side of neck, 6 sts from front neck, 5 sts from other side of neck, 10 sts from sleeve and finally 6 sts from right back (48 sts).

Next row: knit.

Next row: (make ribbon holes) k1, * yfwd, k2tog, rep from * to last st, k1.

Next row: knit.

Cast off.

Shoes

Make two alike, worked in garter stitch.
Using 4.0mm (UK 8, US 6) needles and yarn C cast on 25 sts.
Work 2 rows garter stitch.
Next row: k1, inc in each of next 23 sts, k1 (48 sts).
Join in B and work in garter stitch stripes of 2 rows B and 2 rows C for 12 rows.
Keeping continuity of stripes proceed as follows:
Next row: k9, (k2tog) 15 times, k9 (33 sts).
Next row: knit.
Next row: k9 (k2tog) 7 times, k10 (26 sts).
Next row: knit.
Cast off.

Straps

Make two alike.
Using 4.0mm (UK 8, US 6) needles and yarn C cast on 42 sts.
Knit 2 rows and cast off.
Sew in ends on shoes. Stitch the seam of the shoe, matching up the stripes. Sew the strap to the back of the shoe. Put the shoes onto the rabbit's feet. Overlap the straps at the front and secure with a small button.

Join side and sleeve seams

Thread ribbon through holes at the neck and also at the waist. As a finishing touch, add buttons to the front of the dress, if required.

Bow

Using 4.0mm (UK 8, US 6) needles and yarn B cast on 8 sts, work in garter stitch for 15cm (6in). Cast off. Fold the bow in half and sew the short ends together. Place the join at the centre back. Gather the centre of the piece to form a bow shape. Sew a tiny ribbon bow to the centre of the knitted bow. Sew to the rabbit's head in front of her ears.

Baby Emma

Who will be able to resist this sweet little baby bunny complete with her own tiny onesie? She is made in simple stocking stitch and will only take an evening to knit. I have embroidered little flowers onto the onesie to make it extra special.

Materials
50g (1¾oz) cream DK (8-ply) yarn (A)
50g (1¾oz) sky blue DK (8-ply) yarn (B)
Small amount of black DK (8-ply) yarn
Oddments of pink and green yarn for flower embroidery
Safety stuffing
Small amount of narrow baby ribbon

Needles
4.0mm (UK 8, US 6)

Tension (gauge)
22 sts x 30 rows measures 10 x 10cm (4 x 4in) using 4.0mm (UK 8, US 6) needles over st st

Size
12cm (5in) wide, 26cm (10½in) tall

Body and head
Make in one piece, worked in garter stitch.
Using 4.0mm (UK 8, US 6) needles and yarn A cast on 10 sts.
Next row: purl.
Next row: inc in each st to end (20 sts).
Next row: purl.
Next row: * k1, inc in next st, rep from * to end (30 sts).

Next row: purl.
Work 30 rows in st st (mark this row as neck line).
Continue for a further 16 rows.

Shape top of head
Next row: * k1, k2tog, rep from * to end (20 sts).
Next row: purl.
Next row: (k2tog) across row (10 sts).
Next row: purl.
Next row: (k2tog) five times.
Break yarn, thread through sts on needle, draw up and fasten off.

Arms
Make two alike, worked in garter stitch.
Using 4.0mm (UK 8, US 6) needles and yarn A cast on 7 sts.
Next row: purl.
Next row: inc in each st to end (14 sts).
Next row: purl.
Work 14 rows in st st.
Next row: * k1, inc in next st, rep from * to end (21 sts).
Next row: purl.
Work 4 rows in st st.
Next row: (k2tog) across to last st, k1 (11 sts).
Next row: purl.
Next row: (k2tog) across to last st, k1.
Break yarn and thread through sts, draw up and fasten off.

Ears

Make two alike, worked in garter stitch.
Using 4.0mm (UK 8, US 6) needles and yarn A cast on 6 sts.
Knit 2 rows.
Next row: inc at each end of row (8 sts).
Knit 9 rows.
Next row: k2tog at each end of row (6 sts).
Next row: knit.
Repeat last 2 rows once (4 sts).
Next row: (k2tog) twice.
Next row: k2tog and fasten off.

Legs

Make two alike, worked in garter stitch.
Using 4.0mm (UK 8, US 6) needles and yarn A cast on 7 sts.
Next row: purl.
Next row: inc in each st to end (14 sts).
Next row: purl.
Work 16 rows in st st.

Shape foot

Next row: k4, inc in each of next 6 sts, k4 (20 sts).
Next row: purl.
Work 4 rows in st st.
Next row: (k2tog) across row (10 sts).
Next row: purl.
Repeat last 2 rows once more (5 sts).
Next row: (k2tog) twice, k1 (3 sts).
Break yarn and run through sts on needle. Draw up and fasten off.

Onesie

Knit back and front alike.

Using 4.0mm (UK 8, US 6) needles and yarn B cast on 8 sts.

Work 4 rows in garter stitch.

Change to st st.

Next row: inc 1 st at each end of row (10 sts).

Next row: purl.

Repeat the last 2 rows twice more (14 sts).

Cast on 2 sts at the beg of next 6 rows (26 sts).

Work 24 rows in st st.

Work 8 rows in garter stitch.

Cast off.

To make up bunny and onesie

Begin with the head and body of the bunny. Sew the seam – this runs down the centre back. Leave the base open to stuff. Stuff the head first, making it firm and round. Then take a needle threaded with matching yarn and, beginning at the marked row for the neck, weave the yarn in and out of each stitch all the way around, starting and ending at the seam. Pull up quite firmly and this will form the head and neck. Secure well at the seam. Continue to stuff the body, then close the base. Embroider the rabbit's facial features using black DK (8-ply) yarn.

Pleat the base of the ears, then sew an ear to either side of the top of the head. Sew the arm seams, leaving the top open. Stuff the arms, close the seam, then attach to the shoulders of the bunny on either side. Sew the leg seams, stuff, making sure that you fill out the foot part to give a nice shape. Close the seams then sew the legs to each side of the bunny.

Sew the side seams and crotch of the onesie, remembering to leave a gap at the top on each side to form armholes. Slip onto the bunny. Catch the shoulder seams on either side to form the neck opening.

Thread some coordinating ribbon through the stitches around the centre of the onesie and tie in a pretty bow at the front. Make a small bow from the same ribbon and sew to the top of the head between the ears. Embroider flowers in lazy daisy stitch on the front of the onesie if desired.

Abbreviations

beg	beginning
cm	centimetres
dec	decrease
foll	following
GS	garter stitch
in	inch
inc	increase
k	knit
k2tog	knit 2 stitches together
kfb	knit into front and back of stitch (increasing one stitch)
m1	make a backwards loop on your needle by twisting the yarn towards you and slipping the resulting loop on to the right-hand needle. On the following row, knit or purl through the back of the stitch. This produces a very neat result.
p	purl
p2tog	purl 2 stitches together
psso	pass slipped stitch over
rem	remaining
rep	repeat

RH	right hand
RS	right side
skpo	slip 1 st, knit 1 st, pass slipped st over
sl	slip a stitch
st st	stocking stitch
st(s)	stitch(es)
tbl	through the back of the loop
tog	together
WS	wrong side
yfwd	yarn forward
yo	yarn over needle
yrn	yarn round needle

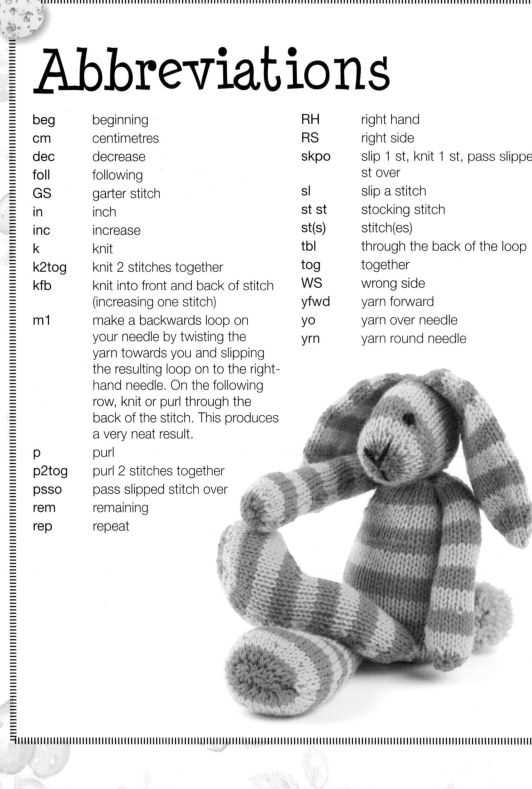